TOWARDS LITURGY 2000

TOWARDS
LITURGY 2000

PREPARING FOR THE REVISION OF THE
ALTERNATIVE SERVICE BOOK

Paul Bradshaw   Mark Dalby   Martin Dudley

Donald Gray   John Fenwick   Derek Pattinson

Michael Perham   Bryan Spinks   Kenneth Stevenson

Edited by
Michael Perham

SPCK/Alcuin Club

First published in Great Britain 1989
for the Alcuin Club by

SPCK
Holy Trinity Church
Marylebone Road
London NW1 4DU

British Library Cataloguing in Publication Data
Perham, Michael
  Towards liturgy 2000.
  1. Church of England. Public worship. Reform
  I. Perham, Michael, 1947—
264'.03

ISBN 0-281-04419-8

Filmset by Pioneer Associates
Printed in Great Britain by the
Bocardo Press Ltd, Didcot

Contents

CONTENTS

The Contributors

Paul Bradshaw is Associate Professor of Liturgy at the University of Notre Dame, Indiana, USA.

Mark Dalby is Team Rector of Worsley in Manchester, and a member of the General Synod and the Liturgical Commission.

Martin Dudley is Vicar of Owlsmoor in Berkshire.

John Fenwick is the Archbishop of Canterbury's Assistant Secretary for Ecumenical Affairs.

Donald Gray is a Canon of Westminster, Rector of St Margaret's Westminster, and Speaker's Chaplain. He is Chairman of the Joint Liturgical Group and the Alcuin Club and President of *Societas Liturgica*.

Derek Pattinson is Secretary General of the General Synod.

Michael Perham is Team Rector of Oakdale in Poole. He is a member of the Liturgical Commission and the Archbishops' Commission on Church Music. He has recently been elected to the General Synod, and is Secretary of the Alcuin Club.

Bryan Spinks is Chaplain of Churchill College, Cambridge, and lectures in liturgy in the University of Cambridge. He is a member of the Liturgical Commission.

Kenneth Stevenson is Rector of Holy Trinity and St Mary's, Guildford, and a member of the Liturgical Commission. He is also Secretary to the Anglo-Scandinavian Theological Conferences.

1

Preparing the Way

DONALD GRAY

It is perhaps not surprising that the Alternative Service Book does not, in its opening pages, supply introductory material that compares with the Book of Common Prayer's section, for instance, on the Golden Number, material which can be used for whiling away periods of enforced boredom during divine worship. Is it because the ASB is confident (some would say overconfident) in its ability to hold and command the attention? But if attention does happen to stray and the eye falls upon page eight, the distracted worshipper would discover, either with joy or despair, that it states there that the authorization for use of the book extends only to the last day of 1990. However the joy would be dampened or the despair lifted by the knowledge that, as yet, few copies of the ASB have been printed with the information that the General Synod, in its wisdom, has subsequently further extended its life to the end of the century, until 31 December 2000.

This decision was made by the Synod after considering a report from its Standing Committee entitled *The Worship of the Church* (published as GS 698 in October 1985). This report, recognizing that, in these days, there could not be a policy of liturgical 'freeze' or 'standstill', recommended a three stage programme in relation to the ASB. First, a programme of teaching and study backed by a 'directory' which would contain 'a wealth of resource material including supplementary material for each of the many points where there is room for the individual's own words', and would also encourage the kind of 'loosening up' in worship that the ASB had in mind.

Secondly, it recommended a thorough and sustained evaluation of the ASB; and thirdly, the preparation, as circumstances required, either of additional material or of substantially new texts. It was in order to give space for these developments that the Synod decided to remove any uncertainty about the future of ASB by extending its period of authorization until the end of the year 2000.

In the meantime the Synod stated that they believed that they should receive periodic progress reports on liturgical business with the intention that there should be a stocktaking during the life of the Synod due to be elected in 1990. It would be at this point that the Synod would decide whether or not to chart a definite course towards a replacement of *ASB 1980*. The General Synod endorsed this as 'a strategy for its own liturgical work and for the work of the Liturgical Commission in the coming years', on 21 November 1985.

The present Liturgical Commission is busily engaged in the preparation of material which might be said to arise out of the first and third of those programme stages but it has not been able to commence work on the detailed evaluation of the ASB. Some may argue that it is still early days for such an assessment, but if the 1990 Synod and its Liturgical Commission are to have the information they need to make a decision 'whether or not to chart a definite course towards a replacement of *ASB 1980*', then the process of evaluation must commence now.

This collection of essays, which it is hoped will start the ball rolling, comes from members of the Alcuin Club. It was not the intention of the Alcuin Club to usurp a responsibility which properly belongs to the Synod and its Liturgical Commission; but rather we believe that, through its reasonably wide membership among the liturgically minded in the Church of England, it can perform a useful service and provide material which can assist a wide discussion of the issues involved in preparing for the year 2000.

This project recalls the positive role the Alcuin Club played more than sixty years ago in the discussion which surrounded the production of the book which is usually referred to as the 1928 Prayer Book.

The background material for that book had begun to be prepared soon after the Royal Letters of Business had been issued at the end of 1906,[1] although it took another six years before anything resembling a Liturgical Commission was formed. It became known as the 'Committee of Experts',[2] but it did not enjoy a long life, holding its last meeting in 1915.[3] So in addition to what was drawn up by the Committees of the Convocations, and later of the Church Assembly, two 'liturgical pressure groups' were formed.

The first of these was the voice of Anglo-Catholicism. In the early stages the English Church Union had shown little or no enthusiasm for Prayer Book revision, knowing that the demand for such proposals stemmed from attempts to suppress many of the liturgical practices they held dear. It was not until 1917 that they decided to contribute to the debate. After a preliminary report in 1919 they issued their recommendations for the revision of proposals currently 'on the table' in the form of a schedule attached to a report. This report predates the 'Green Book' in which those same recommendations were printed out *in extenso*.[4]

Alongside these proposals were those of a group who had been involved in the Life and Liberty Movement. Their proposals were contained in what became known as the 'Grey Books'. The compilers of these books, in contrast with the 'Green Book's' effort to 'build up a really august and majestic English Catholic Rite',[5] believed 'that there is a need for more experiment and freedom in the worship of the Church . . . not only more elasticity in the regular services but also a greater freedom in the services provided'.[6]

It was these three schemes (the 'official', the ECU's 'Green Book' and the more liberal 'Grey Book') of which the Alcuin Club sought to provide a survey in the later volumes of its

Prayer Book Revision Pamphlets. This series had been commenced back in 1912 but at that time had not attempted to make any proposals for revision, noting only that 'whether or not the Book of Common Prayer is revised by this generation or not, nothing but good can come from the spread of sound knowledge upon liturgical subjects'.[7] By 1923 a different mood prevailed.

In October 1923 the Alcuin Club Committee felt the situation regarding Prayer Book revision necessitated a monthly meeting on a fixed day for the following six months! Out of this enhanced activity came three publications, the paperback editions of which were produced, not in 'Alcuin Green' but in orange; hence the Alcuin Club contributions to this colourful debate were, not surprisingly, dubbed the 'Orange Books'. The 'Orange Books' did not set out to add another scheme to the three already available but to suggest ways in which those schemes could be simplified and combined. The Alcuin Club suggested few ideas of its own, although it did, surprisingly, say that it had introduced 'sparingly some modernization of language'.[8]

In this present volume the Alcuin Club is aiming once again to be of service to the Church of England by commencing a process of discussion and debate which will assist it in coming to right decisions about the future forms of its worship. Any such decisions must be taken against the background of sound scholarship, which has always been part of the Alcuin Club's tradition. But such scholarship can never be 'party', and must always run the risk of exploding 'Catholic' myths as well as 'Evangelical' and 'Liberal' myths. Equally, such work must be related not only to the Anglican Communion as a whole, where there are many new and exciting developments, but also to the ecumenical world in which we now live. Liturgy has, for some years, been increasingly an area of generous ecumenical sharing, and this not merely in the realms of scholarship and research but equally in our willingness to use each other's texts and insights.

Historically, the Alcuin Club took its stand against what it believed were the excesses and foreign practices of Rome and the uncritical Romanizers on the one hand, *and* against the reductionist practices of 'Low Church' on the other. In the circumstances of the late nineteenth and early twentieth centuries, this led to the espousal of a moderately Catholic style with an emphasis on its roots in English Church usage. That position has been widely influential, and has helped form and foster an Anglican sense of dignity and beauty in Western-rite worship, without simply aping Rome.

Today we operate in a situation where the perceptions of many at all points in the church spectrum are very different. Catholicism is not about Dearmer-style altars and full surplices, nor is Evangelicalism about north end celebrations. Old shibboleths have been abandoned. Fussy, self-conscious, tightly-choreographed worship is judged as false. There is a general simplification of style. The Middle Ages (or 1549) are no longer seen as the ideal. The spotlight has shifted to the Patristic era, which makes some of the earlier Alcuin publications feel curiously irrelevant.

The Alcuin Club believes that the challenge for today is to identify what is authentic and of permanent value in the tradition, and to feed those insights into the revision process, which will be upon us sooner than we think, in a way that does not look like an obsession with antiquarianism.

Our treatment of the subject is necessarily selective. Six of the chapters (2 and 3, 9 to 12) examine some of the major issues about the basic concept of a new book. The middle chapters (4 to 9) take in turn five particular areas where *ASB 1980* seems to be wearing thin very quickly. Of course there could have been others, though it is significant that, though we have included the Eucharistic Prayer among those five, we have not thought it necessary to include the whole Eucharistic Rite as ripe for a rethink.

We have not attempted to assess how the present Liturgical Commission's material for use particularly in Urban Priority Areas and to enrich the Family Service phenomenon will find a place in a new sort of book, though before the successor to the ASB is even in its first draft the reception to that material will be clear enough for it to exercise a strong influence.

It is not only that this book does not set out to *answer* all the questions. It does not even seek to *ask* them all. But it is a beginning, the beginning of a process of great importance to a Church about to enter a decade of evangelism.

NOTES

1 G. K. A. Bell, *Randall Davidson, Archbishop of Canterbury*, 3rd edn 1952, pp. 649–50.

2 *Minutes of the Advisory Committee in Liturgical Questions Appointed at the Request of the Upper House of the Convocation of Canterbury*, 1st Meeting, Lambeth Palace, Tuesday 22 October 1912. MS 1642 (Jenkins Papers) f. 79, Lambeth Palace Library.

3 R. C. D. Jasper, ed., *Walter Howard Frere His Correspondence on Liturgical Revision and Construction*, ACC no. XXXIX, 1954, p. 55.

4 *A Suggested Prayer Book. Being the text of the English Rite altered and enlarged in accordance with the Prayer Book Revision proposals made by the English Church Union*, 1923.

5 ECU, *Report*, op. cit., p. 3.

6 *The Kingdom, the Power and the Glory, being part III of 'A New Prayer Book' (The 'Grey Book')*, 3rd edn 1925, p. iii.

7 'Note by the Committee', in T. A. Lacey, *Liturgical Interpolations and the Revision of the Prayer Book*, Alcuin Club Prayer Book Revision Pamphlets I, 1912, p. iv.

8 *A Survey of the Proposals for the Alternative Prayer Book, Part 1, The Order of Holy Communion*, Alcuin Club Prayer Book Revision Pamphlets XII, 1923, p. 6.

2

What Kind of Book?

BRYAN SPINKS

In the Pastoral Letter of 16 November 1980 which introduced the ASB, the Archbishops wrote:

> The new book is the culmination of a lively period of liturgical experiment and change. It establishes the liturgy of the Church in a more stable form than we have known for some years.

It cannot be denied that the ASB has established itself firmly in the life of the Church. This has been demonstrated both by the sales of the book, and the surveys undertaken by diocesan liturgical committees, and by the Prayer Book Society, all of which indicate the extent to which the ASB has been a success. It was a wise decision by the General Synod in November 1985 to endorse the recommendation made in GS 698, *The Worship of the Church*, that the date of any revision of the ASB should be 2000 rather than 1990. But what precisely should happen in 2000? Minor emendations or major revisions? And what form should the ultimate revised work take?

It is understandable that there should be a reluctance to give up this popular book and return to a period of instability. If a product is selling well and is popular, why change the product? The thought of a new wave of little experimental books is a prospect which must depress even the most dedicated of liturgical fidgets; and surely the great efforts of the Commissions which culminated in the rites of the ASB are not to be swept away after so short a period? I have some slight sympathy,

7

therefore, with those clergy and laity who urge that the revision in 2000 should be modest. These would urge that all that is needed is a simplification of the presentation, omission of material which seems to be rarely used, a reduction of the contents to make it more manageable (e.g. the Ordinal), and the adoption of 'inclusive' language. Looking back in history, we might compare what is envisaged with the 1662 revision of the 1559 Prayer Book.

However, in my view, there are a number of incontrovertible reasons why the ASB must be thoroughly revised in the year 2000, whatever the initial inconvenience or resistance.

To begin with, Christian liturgy by its very nature is something which ought to change as the Christian community progresses and journeys through God's history. This was true of the early period of church history when prayer was often extempore, but even with the appearance of written forms, development and metamorphosis continued. One need only compare the *Didache* with its revision in Serapion and *Apostolic Constitutions*, or the various anaphoras of St Basil which show rapid theological expansion and change. There is no indication that the Reformers of the Church of England intended that the English liturgy should ever become frozen, and open only to minor modest reform. The 1548 Proclamation spoke of the setting forth from time to time of 'godly orders', and indeed between 1548 and 1662 considerable liturgical changes took place. Only by accident (happy or otherwise) did the 1662 rite survive without official alteration or alternatives, to be given some sort of canonical status in Anglicanism. But it was an accident, parallel perhaps only to the Tridentine rites. There is a danger that the ASB, because it has been successful in the 1980s, will assume a similar role, as though it were yet another 'incomparable liturgy'. As the Church changes, and as a changing society impinges upon the life of Christians, so too forms of worship must develop and change. To make the ASB anything other than provisional, and 'for a time' is to mistake the fundamental nature of liturgy, and to make an accident of Anglican history into a liturgical norm.

A second reason for the need for a proper, comprehensive revision in 2000 stems from the first. For almost 300 years the Church of England had only one idea of liturgical forms — those made by Cranmer and modified in 1662. The BCP was called an 'incomparable' liturgy, but there was never a real chance to compare it with anything else. The 1928 abortive revision, for all its differences, is still in the 1662 mould. Only with the Prayer Book (Alternative and Other Services) Measure, the experimental rites, and the ASB have members of the Church of England been able to experience a different dimension in worship. These provisions were the beginning of a liturgical thaw, and the ASB was not a refreezing of a short spring! We can now view liturgy from a wider perspective, and are in a position to create even more satisfying liturgical forms.

Thirdly, if the Church of England takes scholarship seriously, then present liturgical scholarship demands that the ASB must be properly revised. The Commissions which prepared the ASB rites drew on the best scholarship of the previous thirty to forty years, and on ecumenical insights. But the use of that scholarship and ecumenism was limited to the Eucharist, baptism and ordination. There are few signs of these insights in the Divine Office, the marriage service and the funeral rite — and indeed, members of the Commission have admitted that pressure of time prevented these being tackled at the same level as other rites. The subsequent work on the Divine Office by Mateos, Bradshaw and Taft point to an urgent reform in this area. Kenneth Stevenson's study of marriage rites shows the ASB rite to be weak at many points; and it will look a very bleak rite in the wake of the new English Roman Catholic revisions being compiled now. But even the eucharistic liturgy is dated. The anaphoras reflect the preoccupation of the 1960s with Hippolytus and the Syro-Byzantine pattern. Only now are

older patterns and other patterns being appreciated and
explored. Furthermore, the language of the eucharistic prayers
has tended to follow the fifth-century type of list of salvation
history of the past; only now are we beginning to compose
eucharistic prayers which give thanks for God's salvific work
in the lives of Christians now. The fruits of recent scholarship
must not be ignored, but used for the benefit of the Church.

A fourth important reason for a thorough revision in 2000
is that of liturgical language. Many have complained that the
ASB is dull and flat in comparison with Cranmer's English.
The criticism has been exaggerated; some parts of the ASB
have a great deal of rhythm, and much of 'Cranmer' is in fact
the work of the Restoration divines! However, it is certainly
true that we have not yet created a happy twentieth century (or
twenty-first century) English liturgical style which is evocative.
Gail Ramshaw-Schmidt, writing on recent American revision,
has said:

> The choice for succinct court address as the rhetoric of
> prayer in the west was compounded in recent decades by a
> nearly universal decision to cast contemporary English
> prayers in the terse style and simple vocabulary of freshmen
> compositions. Increasingly liturgists are dissatisfied —
> perhaps also bored — with this concise style of corporate
> prayer. After all, twentieth-century literature has given us
> not only Hemingway, but also Virginia Woolf. It could in
> fact be argued that the passion of prayer requires evocative
> images and embellished phrases, that complex sentences
> need not be obscure, and that the brevity of prayers does not
> necessarily lead to better comprehension.[1]

Here it is not just a matter of tampering with ASB words. A
new style needs to be developed, which will result in evocative
euchology and formulae.

Thus to revise the ASB in a modest fashion simply will not
do if the Church of England is serious about good worship.

The scale of the revision necessary in 2000 will stand to the ASB rather as 1552 did to 1549 (liturgically speaking rather than doctrinally speaking!); the continuity and change will be just as apparent.

Yet if large parts of the ASB need to be taken back to the drawing board, what *format* will the resulting work take? With this question in mind, much has been said of a 'directory'. But what precisely is a 'directory'?

The Church of England already has a type of directory: *Lent, Holy Week, Easter*. The then chairman of the Liturgical Commission commended the book to the Church with the words: 'We are providing a *directory* from which choices may be made. We think of this book as a manual to be used with selectivity, sensitivity and imagination.' The book is essentially one of complete services, printed in such a way that, where finances allowed, a parish would feel it right to purchase a copy for everybody. It can be used as a pew edition. At the same time, however, the rubrics allow for some local variation, initiative and selection; the Introduction itself welcomes on some occasions experimentation and innovation.

However, for some others the word directory implies a resource book for worship leaders, who themselves — possibly with a parish worship group — select material for each service. Such a book would thus be a clergy book, or group book, but not a book for the pew. There are definite advantages with this type of directory. Worship cannot become fossilized, and it allows different material for different types of congregation and community. It may be that the Church of England will wish to issue some sort of resource book such as this, but in my opinion such a book would be a *supplement* to the book of 2000, and not the form of 2000 itself. There are, I think, a number of reasons why the Church of England still needs to have a book; though the book may be more like *Lent, Holy Week, Easter* than a Book of Common Prayer.

First, although a *fossilized* liturgy is an accident of Anglican history, it is quite legitimate to argue that an important norm of Anglicanism has been a book of common prayers which is available as much to parishioners as to the priest.

Secondly, there is a certain security in having a book rather than a perpetual series of pamphlets or worship sheets. There is a certain dignity and seriousness in a book, and it provides the *stabilitas* that is necessary for new liturgies to be *prayed* and become part of the spirituality of the Church. The 1662 book was a book of common *prayer*, rather than of common services, and it really could claim to be that because people used their prayer books within their personal prayers. Sometimes it made, no doubt, for too much 'saying of prayers' and too little 'praying', but on the whole it made for a creative relationship between the corporate and the personal. We need to help people to regain that sense of a prayer book, usable at home as well as taken to church, and that necessitates a people's prayer book, rather than a leader's resource book. Only that way can liturgy and spirituality really go hand in hand.

Another reason for a book is that in the Anglican tradition, where liturgy more than doctrinal confession is what holds us in unity, this is very important. A resource book by itself would seriously weaken even further the concept of common Anglican liturgical prayer.

Finally, a resource book presupposes a high degree of liturgical expertise or creativity amongst the clergy, and a reasonably articulate congregation. At the moment many of the older clergy (and alas some of the younger clergy) seem unable to grasp the flexibility of the ASB, and the need for a different presentation from the Prayer Book services; nor at the moment has the Church of England been prepared to finance any serious Liturgical Formation programme to help them. Quite bluntly, by the year 2000 we shall still as a Church be trying to master the flexibility of the ASB and *Lent, Holy Week, Easter*, and could not even begin to handle resource

12

book worship as anything more than an occasional undertaking!

The Church of England needs an alternative prayer book, different in many ways from the ASB, but evolving from it. There may be some resource collection as a supplement; but the revision of 2000 will produce a book. Pastoral, liturgical and doctrinal needs all point in this direction.

NOTE

1 Gail Ramshaw-Schmidt, 'Our Final Praise: The Concluding Doxology', in Frank C. Senn, ed., *New Eucharistic Prayers*, New York: Paulist Press 1987, pp. 210–13, 211–12.

3

Worship in the Spirit

JOHN FENWICK

The process of revision of the ASB leading up to the year 2000 contains a new factor that was not present in the 1920s, or even (in any sizeable form) in the 1960s and early 1970s — the charismatic movement. For good or ill the movement has spread widely and deeply in parts of the Church of England and is now firmly part of the ecclesiastical scene (there are 'charismatic' members of both the House of Bishops and the Alcuin Club!).

This is not the place to recount the history and characteristics of the charismatic movement, but if the Alcuin Club is to enter realistically into the debates preceding the revision of ASB, it has to accept the fact that thousands of English Anglicans and hundreds, if not thousands, of Church of England parishes and clergy have had their lives profoundly affected by a powerful experience which they believe is of the Holy Spirit. The movement has matured considerably since its early days. There is less insistence on the necessity of a single experience of 'baptism in the Holy Spirit', less insistence on speaking in tongues, and a more eirenic approach to other forms of spiritual experience and growth. Nevertheless, it remains true that there is a divide of sorts between individuals and parishes that are 'into renewal' and those that are not.

As is well known and well documented, the movement's most visible impact has been upon worship. The effects range from a loosening up, the adoption of new music and greater participation through to the exercise of various gifts such as prophecy or tongues, a time of 'ministry' which may include

15

counselling with laying on of hands, healing or 'slaying in the Spirit'. A key concept is that worship should be 'in the Spirit' or 'Spirit-led'. This concept requires some 'unpacking'. All Christians, presumably, would want to talk of the Holy Spirit's involvement in an act of worship as beginning with the preacher's preparation in the study, the choir practice, the rehearsal (if any), and the individual preparation of all who assemble, bearing fruit in an individual and corporate apprehension of the presence of God in the act of worship. Without wishing to deny this dimension, many in the charismatic movement would expect the Spirit's activity to manifest itself in the act of worship by interjecting ingredients or phenomena for which there had been no prior preparation — *for no prior preparation could have been possible*. The inspiration of a worshipper to share a vision or a prophecy, the gift of a 'word of knowledge' to someone present, the moving of the congregation to begin singing in tongues — these are things that cannot be 'scripted in' in advance. There is, clearly, then the potential for a sharp divide between those for whom worship is a spontaneous, God-given encounter, and those who believe it is possible in the mid 1990s to determine substantially the form and content of the worship on, say, the 7th Sunday after Pentecost in the year 2006.

Some have felt the divide between the two conceptions so keenly as to have changed their denominational allegiance. Many formerly loyal Anglicans have joined the House Churches precisely because they found the style of worship in their parish churches too rigid to allow the Spirit to work. And not a few who remain in the Anglican fold sympathize with them. Others have remained in our parishes, convinced that a synthesis of the liturgical and charismatic is possible and, indeed, desirable. Theirs must be an important voice in the years ahead.

So what are the challenges posed by the charismatic

movement to the Church of England in the lead up to revised ASB that will appear in 2000?

1. *To concentrate on essentials*

Liturgical concerns inevitably and rightly have a large conservative component. Liturgy, after all, is one of the marks of the continuity of the Church. But we can never go back and recreate a past age. This is as true for the charismatic who wishes to recreate what he imagines to be the worship of the church of Corinth of AD 50 (without, of course, its problems) as it was for former generations of the Alcuin Club who wished to recreate what they imagined to be the worship of 1549. God calls his people *on*, in continuity with the past. This has the rather disturbing implication that things that were once very important cease to be so, or are important in a different way. There is a curious mixture of openness and intolerance abroad. We live in a time when, partly as a result of the charismatic movement, Catholics and Evangelicals within the Church of England are more open than perhaps ever before to each other's strengths and insights; but there is also a great impatience with each other's shibboleths. Few things close an Evangelical's mind to the glories of the Catholic tradition faster than listening in to a heated vestry discussion about some obtuse detail of ceremonial. We need to make sure that our contribution to the revision of ASB debate concentrates on essential and not peripheral matters and is free from a nostalgic harking back to some unobtainable 'good old days'.

2. *To learn from its paradoxes*

It is easy to caricature some aspects of worship associated with the charismatic movement and its influence. Congregations sing choruses like 'Majesty' but often address God with great familiarity and mateyness and are sloppy in their attention to detail. It is claimed that worship is Spirit-led, but a pattern is soon discernible to the regular attender. Does the term 'liturgical president' really mean no more than that the vicar should have the skills of a television chat-show host ('Mike, I want you to come up here and tell us a little about yourself . . .')? Does Jesus' injunction to worship 'in spirit and in truth' necessarily mean in plain surroundings and with applause and laughter?

Yet the answer is not to condemn too quickly in haughty disdain. We are all too painfully aware of the liturgically-correct but almost empty church, and the assembly which breaks all the rules yet is packed to the doors, vibrant with life, and composed of people of all ages who have a life-changing knowledge of God. As the Alcuin Club is not in itself an agent of the renewal movement, perhaps the challenge here focuses on its *teaching* role. Do we need to be arguing strongly for the revised ASB to be accompanied by a realistic and pastorally sensitive equivalent of the Roman General Instruction? The Church of England has a history of producing liturgical texts with little or no aid to presbyter or people as to how they might be implemented or integrated into pastoral practice. Such provision might reduce some of the sloppiness, misunder-standing and liturgical howlers that are all too apparent. But we need to have the humility to recognize that it will not, of itself, bring spiritual life, and perhaps the Club needs to urge the Church of England to address liturgically-based spiritual formation as part of its agenda, or to be ready to step into the breach if official provision fails.

It was in an Alcuin Club publication that the present writer first discovered the description of St Basil of Caesarea's uttering of the epiclesis as being like Elijah calling down fire on Mount Carmel. Basil, the evidence suggests, spent a lot of time concentrating on the details of textual amendment, but he also seems to have remembered the Pneumatic element. Perhaps what our generation needs is more Spirit-filled liturgists on the Liturgical Commission and in our parishes.

4

Initiation

MARK DALBY

The Initiation Services have been described as the least satisfactory part of ASB. In view of the Church of England's continuing confusion on so many aspects of initiation, this is hardly surprising. None the less ASB has now 'institutionalized' some of this confusion, and even added to it.

In the table of contents, Initiation Services involve 16 sections, and at least 3 of these should not have been included here. Thanksgiving for the Birth of a Child and Thanksgiving after Adoption are pastoral offices sometimes used in their own right but sometimes commended as alternatives to initiation. They are rightly included in the book, but they are no part of initiation. The Renewal of Baptismal Vows is another useful provision (though some find it rather bare), but again it is not — as presented here — an initiation service.

As against ASB, the Book of Common Prayer included only four 'initiation services', and these included the Catechism which ASB omits. Some might argue that a catechism has no place in initiation services, but instruction has been linked with initiation from the very beginning, and the presence of a catechism in close association with the initiation services is witness to the importance of this link. ASB's omission of a catechism is understandable. *The Revised Catechism* of 1962 antedated the present phase of liturgical reform. It was based firmly on its Prayer Book original, and though at some points it went considerably beyond it, it included formularies like the Creed and Lord's Prayer in their Prayer Book form and liturgically it reflected the ethos of Series One or Two or

19

ASB's Rite B. ASB could of course have made minor amendments to its language and amended its formularies to conform to its own usage, but many members of General Synod wanted a more radical revision, and there was not the time, or perhaps the will, to produce this. None the less a revised ASB must surely include a catechism, and since (as I shall show) neither of the present catechisms can be used satisfactorily with ASB, either they or preferably ASB will have to be drastically amended.

The main body of ASB's Initiation Services contains minor irritants as well as more glaring deficiencies. Examples of the former include:

(a) Family Baptism. The second rubric states strangely that 'Where children who are old enough to respond are baptised, the parents and godparents answer the questions, and, at the discretion of the priest, the children also may answer them.' It is remarkable, to say the least, that children old enough to respond may do so only 'at the discretion of the priest', and it would be interesting to see a theological or liturgical defence of this provision.

(b) The Signing with the Cross. This may now take place either after the profession of faith (and before the baptism) where the formula is printed in full or, as in the Book of Common Prayer, immediately after the baptism. There is good precedent for a signing at each position, and it would have been good if ASB had allowed this. As it is, we now have to choose between them, and those who prefer to use an official booklet or card find it difficult to have the signing in the Prayer Book position since the full text is printed only in the earlier position. This practical abolition of the Prayer Book's post-baptismal signing represents the removal of one of our neighbours' most familiar liturgical landmarks.

(c) Emergency Baptism. Rubric 106 states that the parents are responsible for requesting this. But where the parents do not request it, many clergy and even hospital sisters would deem it their responsibility to suggest it to them. ASB is so anxious to assert that 'questions of ultimate salvation' do not depend on whether or not a child has been baptized that it seems to be minimizing the traditional necessity of baptism.

Many liturgists would regard ASB's ambiguities on anointing as among its major deficiencies, but oil has been an emotive subject in the Church of England, and since the Book of Common Prayer made no provision at all for anointing we should probably be grateful for what ASB does allow: an anointing with the sign of the cross before *or* after (but not, as traditionally, before *and* after) baptism, and again at the laying on of the bishop's hand at confirmation. ASB's reference to the Blessing of the Oils (plural) on Maundy Thursday implies a recognition of the three traditional oils: the oil of catechumens, the oil of the sick and chrism. If the sign of the cross is made before baptism, the oil of catechumens should be used; if it is made after baptism, it should be made with chrism. But it is probably better not to use oil at all at baptism unless it is also likely to be used at confirmation, since the anointing (with chrism) at confirmation is the most important of the three anointings.

It would be helpful if a revised ASB could offer more guidance here. It should certainly make provision for all three traditional initiatory anointings, and it would be good, not least on ecumenical grounds, if the use of oil became an invariable feature at confirmation. In other respects, though, the ASB Confirmation rite is a good one, and the phrase in the bishop's prayer, 'Let your Holy Spirit rest upon them', represents a positive compromise between the different views of the Spirit's role in confirmation.

The really glaring deficiencies of ASB relate not to confirmation but to baptism, and they derive essentially from its treatment of adult baptism as the norm. Aidan Kavanagh has pointed out that

A norm in this sense has nothing to do with the number of times a thing is done, but it has everything to do with the standard according to which a thing is done . . . The normal as defined by tradition is differentiated from the usual as defined by convention.[1]

But in opting for adult baptism as 'the normal as defined by tradition' ASB has ignored the warnings of A. R. Vidler:

It is sometimes supposed that because Christian initiation was originally received only or mainly by adults, therefore infant baptism, however justifiable, entails a departure from what must be theologically normative. But it is equally possible, and perhaps more reasonable, to regard the New Testament period as in this respect abnormal and exceptional. Not until families and nations were Christian could Christian initiation assume its normal form.[2]

Vidler was right to see *infant* baptism, not *adult*, as 'the normal as defined by tradition'. As for 'the usual as defined by convention', despite the decline in the visible observance of Christianity in England, infant baptism is still far more common than adult baptism. In 1985 there were 201,000 baptisms in the Church of England of infants under one year of age as against 38,000 other baptisms.[3] There is no wholly reliable way of calculating the ages of these 38,000 others, but there are good grounds for thinking that only a quarter or so were old enough to answer for themselves. This would make about 230,000 infant and child baptisms as against 10,000 adolescent and adult baptisms.

The Episcopal Church in the USA and the Anglican Church of Canada have both produced single rites for adults and infants alike, but *An Australian Prayer Book* of 1978 places infant baptism first, while the Church of Ireland's *Alternative Prayer Book 1984* includes only infant baptism. *The Methodist Service Book* of 1975 places infant baptism first, and so too does *The Book of Common Order* issued by the Church of Scotland in 1979. From the Roman Catholic side, the publication of a new *Rite of Christian Initiation of Adults* in 1972 was seen by Kavanagh as 'the definitive statement of what the Roman Catholic Church's *norm of baptism* is henceforth to be',[4] but it was partly to counteract such statements that in 1980 the Vatican issued an *Instruction on Infant Baptism* which re-emphasized that infant baptism was still 'a general rule' and 'a serious duty'.[5]

ASB represents not a general consensus but merely a transatlantic trend, and by providing the great majority of its candidates for baptism, i.e. infants, with a rite which was ultimately designed for others, i.e. adults, it fails both pastorally and liturgically. Some of the pastoral consequences of this have been described by Wesley Carr.[6] One of the liturgical consequences is the disappearance of any reference to the story of the Lord's blessing of the children. Jasper and Bradshaw state that 'it is now generally recognised as not referring to Baptism',[7] a judgement which would surprise both Cullmann and Jeremias, though in ASB's strange exegesis it must refer to Thanksgiving for the Birth of a Child, Thanksgiving after Adoption and the Funeral of a Child, since it is still read on each of these occasions. Once again ASB is very much alone. The story is omitted in the Canadian baptismal rite, but it is one of several authorized gospel readings in the Roman Catholic rite and in the rites of Australia, Ireland and the United States. It is a compulsory reading in the Church of Scotland and the Methodist Church.

Just how radically ASB has departed from the Anglican tradition in all this is immediately apparent if we consider how radically an ASB-type catechism would have to differ from its predecessors. Our present catechisms assume that baptism has already taken place, and they begin with our godparents, the benefits of the baptism which they sought for us and the promises which they made for us. An ASB-type catechism, however, would have to assume absurdly that the normal recipient of catechesis in England was an adult who had not yet been baptized. It would require a wholly different starting point.

There could of course be two catechisms, one for unbaptized adults and one for baptized children, and perhaps a third for adults who had been baptized but not confirmed. But even an ASB-type catechism for baptized children or adolescents would have to begin very differently from its predecessors. In the Book of Common Prayer the emphasis is on the godparents who express the faith of the Church. It is the godparents who are referred to in the Catechism, and it was not until the passing of the Prayer Book (Further Provisions) (No. 2) Measure in 1968 that the presence of the parents was even required at the service. Now, however, in ASB the parents are not merely required to be present but have to state their willingness to provide help and encouragement by prayers, example and teaching, and they have to join in The Decision and the profession of faith along with the godparents. No one today would criticize the desire for the parents to be present, but what if only one parent is a believer? What if neither is a believer, but there is a believing grandparent or godparent who can influence the child? Strictly speaking ASB would deny baptism in these cases. It seeks to make baptism conditional on the faith of the parents in a way that even Calvin would not have done, while Whitgift and Hooker would turn in their graves.

ASB would also require the deletion from the Catechism of any reference to the baptismal promise. Our present catechisms have a twofold purpose. They are an exposition of our threefold baptismal promise (with an appendix on the sacraments) *and* a renewal of that promise: 'Dost thou not think that thou art bound to believe, and to do, as they have promised for thee? Yes verily; and by God's help so I will.' In the Book of Common Prayer the renunciation and the obedience have a future as well as a present reference — 'all the days of thy life'. But though ASB has its form for The Renewal of Baptismal Vows which speaks clearly of 'promises', its actual baptismal rite contains no vows or promises of any kind. The answers in The Decision and in the profession of faith are made by parents and godparents for the children as well as for themselves, but they are made in the present tense with no future reference. ASB has avoided the problem of promises made for the future by third parties by accentuating the equal problem of categorical statements about the child's present faith. Paradoxically the problems are less when both emphases are held together, as in the Prayer Book, than when one is stressed to the exclusion of the other as in ASB. But if ASB is deficient here we can hardly be surprised. It does not really believe in infant baptism in the way that the Church of England has hitherto believed in it and that most members of the Church of England still believe in it. ASB 2000 has a lot to put right.[8]

NOTES

1 *The Shape of Baptism: The Rite of Christian Initiation*, New York 1978, pp. 108ff.
2 *The Theology of F. D. Maurice*, London 1948, p. 98.
3 *1987 Church Statistics*, London, CIO, p. 8.
4 'The New Roman Rites of Adult Initiation', *Studia Liturgica* X (1974), p. 35.
5 London, Catholic Truth Society 1980, pp. 9 and 14.
6 *Brief Encounters*, London, SPCK 1985, pp. 63–85, esp. pp. 77–82.
7 *A Companion to the Alternative Service Book*, London, SPCK 1986, p. 350.
8 The difference in attitude to infant baptism between BCP and ASB is very considerable, and I have dealt with this more fully in *Open Baptism*, SPCK 1989.

5

The Daily Office

PAUL BRADSHAW

The Preface to the 1549 Book of Common Prayer declared that the primary purpose of Morning and Evening Prayer was understood to be to provide a simple and uniform pattern of daily Bible reading, whereby

> the Clergy . . . should (by often reading, and meditation in God's word) be stirred up to godliness themselves, and be the more able to exhort others by wholesome doctrine, and to confute them that were adversaries to the truth: and further, that the people (by daily hearing of holy Scripture read in the Church) might continually profit more and more in the knowledge of God, and be the more inflamed with the love of his true religion.

The services themselves confirm this to be the aim. Although they contain other elements — the offering of praise in the canticles, and petition in the Lord's Prayer, preces, and collects — they centre around the consecutive reading of the Bible, in which the Old Testament was completed once each year and the New Testament three times, with the exception of the Book of Revelation. The Psalter too was recited in its biblical order in the course of each month, and these cycles were interrupted by 'proper' psalms and readings only on the most important festivals.

Later revisions of the Prayer Book did not significantly alter this focus. A penitential introduction was added to the services in 1552; in 1559 proper lessons were provided for all major feasts, and proper first lessons for every Sunday; and additional prayers were appended to the services in 1662. The regular cycles of psalmody and scriptural readings, however, still constituted the heart of the Offices, and even later revisions of the lectionary did not depart from the principle of the consecutive reading of the whole Bible. The 1871 revision simply reduced the length of the passages to be read on each occasion, and the revisions of 1922, 1947, and 1955 chiefly tried to some extent to match the distribution of the biblical material to the progression of the liturgical year, whilst continuing in general to adhere to the idea of reading each book in order.

Moreover, the recitation of the Psalter in essentially its biblical order, and the reading of the other books of the Bible in a consecutive manner, still form the nucleus of recent revisions of the daily Office both in the Alternative Service Book and throughout the Anglican Communion. The quantity of material used at each service has been considerably reduced, with the psalmody now spread over longer periods than a month and the rest of Scripture usually distributed over a two-year cycle, but the concept has nowhere been abandoned. Indeed, the Church of England Liturgical Commission declared in 1968 that 'no reviser would wish to depart from the principles enumerated in the Preface to the first Book of Common Prayer'.

Nevertheless, two objections may be raised to the foundation upon which the Anglican Offices rest. The first is purely pragmatic: they have never really worked. With rare exceptions, lay people have not joined with the clergy in their daily celebration, as the 1549 Prayer Book hoped, nor have many used them as the basis for their daily devotions at home. At best, they have provided suitable liturgical forms for Sunday services of the Word. The clergy too have not generally found them attractive vehicles for their daily prayer, as is evidenced throughout their history by the frequent criticism raised against them, the widespread neglect of the obligation to recite them, and the continual search for alternatives to them. Nor has the problem been solved by the advent of the recent revisions. The symptoms of spiritual indigestion may have been treated, but the root cause of the condition still remains. The burden of the heavy scriptural diet has been lightened by spreading it more thinly over a longer period of time and the fare has been rendered a little less monotonous by the provision of different canticles for each day of the week, but this amounts only to the sugar-coating of a bitter pill, and there is little to suggest that the prayer-life of the Anglican clergy has thereby been revitalized.

To this may be added a second, more theological, objection. Whilst meditation on Scripture is a vital part of every Christian's spiritual formation, and it is therefore eminently desirable for the Church to make provision for a systematic programme of Bible study for all its members, this is not the heart of Christian prayer. That instead should be occupied by *eucharistia*, the offering of praise and thanksgiving for what God has done in Christ and, arising from that, of prayer for the consummation of the Kingdom of heaven. Though this receives its fullest manifestation in the eucharistic prayer itself, it is not confined to that but should shape all Christian praying; for it is the liturgical expression of the vocation of the Church to be a royal priesthood, participating in the priesthood of Christ by continually offering the sacrifice of praise to God on behalf of all creation and interceding for the salvation of the whole world.

It is of course *possible* to do this sort of praying through the medium of the traditional Anglican Offices — but only with difficulty. The elements of praise and intercession are insufficiently prominent in the textual material itself for them to be easily seen as the central focus of the activity, and one has therefore frequently to resort to a sort of ecclesiastical double-think, such as, 'When I am reciting this psalm which requests deliverance from my enemies, what I am really doing is interceding on their behalf.' Thus, however hard it is to contemplate modifying a liturgical structure which has characterized Anglicanism for so many centuries, it may be necessary in order to allow the more central aspects of Christian prayer to find a fuller expression, in the same way as the traditional Anglican rites for the Eucharist and for Christian Initiation were reformed in the Alternative Service Book in order to bring out neglected dimensions of those sacramental actions.

What is needed in this case just as much as in those is not an abandoning of tradition but a return to an older stratum of it. As the 1549 Preface reveals, those who framed the orders of Morning and Evening Prayer genuinely thought that they were restoring the most ancient form of the daily Office which had been distorted and corrupted by medieval accretions. Because of the limitations of their historical knowledge and perspective, however, they were only able to trace its evolution back to the beginnings of the monastic movement in the fourth century, and indeed it was not until the middle of the twentieth century that liturgical scholars were able to discern that this form of daily prayer, centred around the recitation of the whole Psalter and the systematic reading of the rest of the Bible, was itself a radical departure from what the Church as a whole had been doing in its daily worship prior to the fourth century, and was continuing to do in places unaffected by the emerging monastic communities.

Future revisions, therefore, would do well to look to a more ancient, and biblical, concept and form of daily prayer, which centred instead around *eucharistia*, with its two interrelated priestly themes: the offering of praise and thanksgiving, and the making of intercession for the world. How might these elements then be expressed? Traditionally the former consisted of certain psalms of praise together with canticles, both non-canonical compositions as well as biblical songs. Thus, for example, Pss. 148–150 rapidly became established as the universal morning song of praise, often together with the Gloria in Excelsis, while the hymn 'Hail, gladdening light' was a common evening canticle. Although the ancient practice was to use the same psalms and hymns every day without variation, except for Sundays and major feasts, there is no reason for twentieth-century Christians to be so limited in their selection, especially as we have inherited such a rich variety of suitable material. However, it does seem worth preserving the principle that its distribution should not be random, but rather reflect appropriateness to the time of day, the day of the week, and the liturgical season. Primitive tradition, for example, reserved the Benedicite to Sundays, since the first day of the week was seen as a commemoration of creation; it would not have regarded it as equally suitable for a Tuesday.

In the course of history the intercessory element in the daily Office has shrunk to be no more than a few generic petitions, as for example, 'O Lord, save your people', and has lost the extensive and more specific biddings which once preceded them. Their former fullness therefore needs to be restored, so that they more closely resemble the prayers of the people in the eucharistic rite, with which they share a common origin. Moreover, if Christian prayer is truly to be priestly, they must be for others and not for ourselves: we pray the Office not for our own spiritual advancement, but for the coming of God's Kingdom and the salvation of the whole world. Intercession is thus not an 'optional extra' which may, if desired, be tacked on to the end; it is of its very essence.

Should the reading of Scripture therefore have no place in the daily Office? By no means; but there is a difference between its reading for the purpose of study and meditation and its proclamation in a liturgical context, where its function is primarily anamnetic, to recall what God has done for our salvation and so lead us to offer praise. All Scripture is suitable for instruction, but not every scriptural passage is equally appropriate for this purpose. To be effective in this, readings will need to be selective rather than consecutive, and subordinate in length and position to the act of praise to which they relate. Primitive tradition seems generally to have reserved the reading of Scripture for services of the Word or other gatherings for instruction rather than for the daily prayers, and to have preferred to use psalms for this anamnetic function. The reason for this was that early Christians viewed the Psalter as specially inspired by the Holy Spirit and as a prophetic book speaking of Christ. For them, therefore, the reading of the psalms offered the best way to encounter their living Lord; but twentieth-century Christians are more likely to find other parts of Scripture, especially the Gospels, more suitable for this purpose, and to be much more selective in their use of psalms, whether as part of this ministry of the Word or as songs of praise.

Nevertheless, getting the right contents in the daily Office is not the whole story. Christians have to pray in widely differing contexts, and although the ideal expression of the prayer of the Church may be an assembly of the whole local congregation under the presidency of its ordained ministers and with strong musical resources, that will rarely be practicable. What is provided, therefore, needs to be flexible enough to encourage a full liturgical celebration where this is possible, but also to be satisfactory when prayed by individuals on their own. Traditional Anglican forms tend to fall somewhere between these two extremes. On the one hand, because of their responsive nature, they do not lend themselves very easily to being prayed by individuals, and on the other hand, for *celebration* instead of mere *recitation*, they need to include action and not just words. This might include ritual movement, the symbolic use of light and perhaps incense, as in ancient times, and attention to appropriate forms of opening and closing the assembly (possibly the kiss of peace for the latter); and also the provision of musical settings in the order of service itself, which are both suitable for congregational singing and appropriate to the specific text. To alternate verses from side to side does not always fit either the nature of the worshipping group or the character of the psalm being sung.

6

The Lectionary

MARTIN DUDLEY

If it was left to the parish priest or worship group to choose the readings for each Sunday's services, there would be as many lectionaries as there are parishes. Yet it is likely that certain patterns of common readings would emerge as the compilers looked back to historic lectionaries or chose readings thematically linked to the liturgical celebrations of the Christian calendar. And for the rest the lections would reflect the needs of the parish and the preferences of the priest and others responsible for worship. This tension between the traditional and that which speaks directly to contemporary need is clearly reflected in liturgical renewal and not least in the introduction of new calendar and lectionary schemes, a prominent yet undervalued feature of it. And the tension continues in the current evaluation of calendars and lectionaries.

After a series of experiments, two lectionary schemes or families of lectionaries have predominated. The first is that which takes its origin from the Joint Liturgical Group (JLG) and which is found in the Alternative Service Book (ASB). The other springs from the post-Vatican II Roman Catholic lectionary, now found in the American Book of Common Prayer of the Episcopal Church and in the Common Lectionary (CL) proposed by the Consultation on Common Texts. Both of them begin from a version of the traditional Western calendar but followed significantly different tracks and both families have developed since the debate in the General Synod in February 1977, when Dean Jasper offered an impassioned defence of the JLG/ASB scheme against the Roman/Episcopal

35

Church scheme. Neither, of course, represents a definitive or near perfect arrangement. No scheme can be allowed to dismantle the traditional structure of the liturgical year, with its deeply rooted associations, and reconstruct it in a way that makes lectionary construction easier. As Dean Jasper said introducing that debate, there is no single right set of principles for such construction; one can construct all kinds of lectionaries on all kinds of principles. So the question cannot be, 'Is this the right structure?' but, 'Does it work? Is it effective for the proclamation of the gospel?'

In part, the answer as far as ASB is concerned has been 'No'. The complaint has been made that the thematic approach does not work and that it distorts the scriptural pattern rather than reflecting and enhancing it, that the lections are often too long, sometimes substantially longer than CL, and that too much use is made of the prophets and of St John's Gospel. The two-year cycle, without continuous reading of books, also leads to some remarkable omissions, it is said. Some of these criticisms have been overcome by supplementing the Sunday eucharistic lectionary of the JLG family with its two-year cycle, with additional options for Holy Week and Easter and proposed for Advent to Candlemas which are rooted in the CL pattern, on a three-year cycle. Complementary to the Sunday eucharistic lectionary is that for Morning Prayer on Sundays, again on a two-year cycle, which follows the JLG Additional Lectionary produced in 1969 and authorized for use in 1971. This provision has been supplemented by lections for Evening Prayer and there are further provisions for readings and psalms for the offices and Eucharist on weekdays, festivals and Holy Days, not envisaged by JLG.

Partly the ASB Calendar and Lectionary failed precisely because they were not bold enough. An example of this is the underlying structure of the JLG/ASB Lectionary, a version of the traditional Western calendar which differs from that employed by Rome and in the CL in more than the obvious difference of names given to the Sundays. The JLG scheme has four periods: the nine Sundays before Christmas, where the story of the creation, the fall, and the saving purposes of God as revealed in the Hebrew Scriptures (which provide the controlling reading), sets the scene for the Incarnation; Christmas to Easter, where the gospel reading controls and sets out the life and ministry of Jesus in more or less chronological order; Easter to Pentecost, when the gospel reading still controls and where the resurrection appearances are presented in one year and the concepts of eternal life in the Johannine 'I am' passages in the other; and finally the Sundays after Pentecost. These periods are controlled theologically rather than liturgically and offer a more didactic approach to Christian worship. The periods and their themes offered new opportunities for systematic preaching and teaching, but not enough was made of them. Afraid of the charge that they had allowed themes to dictate readings, the compilers played the themes down and they are hidden on page 1092 in ASB. A bolder use of the thematic approach, though open to criticism, might have been more robust in the face of it.

The question that now emerges is whether the JLG/ASB lectionary should be abandoned in favour of a version closer to CL. As a question it emerges from liturgical circles. Parishes are more likely to stick with the lectionary, albeit with complaint, or to modify and supplement it according to local necessity. Liturgical change has close similarities to other sorts of change, and to be of lasting effect it needs a shift of paradigms, of the basic concepts and structures that control our view of things. A system that will ultimately be seen to be unsatisfactory will not as a general rule be replaced wholesale but modified piecemeal. Liturgists knew and know now why they wanted change. They could justify that change both liturgically and theologically. They expected Anglican Christians to be 'formed by the way in which they pray' and acted accordingly. Yet though the change from the constant Sunday

readings of the Book of Common Prayer and Missal to a two-
or three-year cycle was little short of revolutionary, it did not
reflect a general desire for change by the majority of church-
going Christians and it appears to have had little effect on their
formation as Christians. Indeed loss was more obvious than
gain, for there is an undeniable power in the hearing of the
same Epistle and Gospel on a given Sunday year after year, a
power amplified by it being always heard in the same
translation. The resonances created by language and texts
frequently repeated should not be underestimated. It is true
that only a small amount of Scripture is heard in that way and
with few people attending more than one service a week the
Sunday eucharistic lections, or Mattins readings, were not
supplemented and many major passages went unread and
unheard. But what was used was well known, frequently known
by heart and well loved. There is no evidence to suggest that
this loss was compensated for by a movement towards general
liturgical renewal or by a renewal in the biblical apostolate
such as that experienced in parts of the Roman Catholic
Church. On the Continent especially, it was this return to
Scripture as a feature of spirituality and pastoral care that
created the desire for the increased range and diversity of
lections offered by a three-year cycle of three readings a Sunday.
It may be an academic exercise, another rearrangement of the
deckchairs on the Titanic, for the Church to restructure the
lections before it has taken mission and church-growth seriously.

The most obvious change to the traditional calendar
implemented in ASB was the extension of the pre-Christmas
period from four Sundays to nine. Yet that extension and the
change of emphasis it involved was also minimized by keeping
the changes of the liturgical colour to violet for Advent Sunday.
Instead of that the new approach should have been stressed
and there should have been suggestions for appropriate
thematic ritual celebrations which would have made the
theological scheme of the lectionary and, more importantly, its

content clearer. The history of the Church's year shows that such change is not unprecedented in the West for it reveals much greater diversity and development than might be expected. So in Rome the year first began in March and ended in February. Then the Old Gelasian Sacramentary (dated between 628 and 715) placed its beginning on 25 December and ending on 24 December. Advent developed in imitation of Lent perhaps in the sixth century. In the eighth or ninth century the year started on the first Sunday of Advent, though the number of Sundays in Advent varied before becoming fixed at four in the Gregorian books and for the rest of the Middle Ages.

There were also variations at the other end of the calendar from which JLG might have learned. In the seventh century in Rome the season after Pentecost was not treated as a single unit but divided into five groups each dependent on a fixed major festival: five Sundays after Pentecost; five after St Peter and St Paul; five after St Lawrence (10 August); nine after the Holy Angel (29 September), and then the four Sundays of Advent. The Frankish Gelasian sacramentaries of the late eighth century had twenty-six to twenty-seven Sundays after Pentecost and five *ante Natale Domini*. Whilst no single pattern is necessarily more correct than another, new patterns emerge not only for theological and liturgical reasons but also in response to changes in the civil year, such as altered Bank Holidays, half term, change of clocks, etc., and the times of work and holiday. The variation in sequence after Pentecost might suggest that a similar pattern of linked units of five Sundays, marked by liturgical differentiation, would be a more effective way of coping with a prolonged and unwieldy interval marked by frequent holiday periods.

The Liturgical Commission is already responding to another concern, that for liturgy in Urban Priority Areas and among groups of people who are not accustomed to handling literary texts. A stress is laid on the concrete and the tangible as the concern of UPA people rather than the abstract and theoretical. To respond to this, worship, and especially liturgical readings, need to emphasize history, story, and narrative. Marcan parables and miracles are therefore to be preferred to the great discourses of John 14–17 so beloved of the ASB Lectionary. The Commission that produced *Faith in the City* looked for a liturgy that would 'reflect a universality of form with local variations' and would allow 'significant space for worship which is genuinely local, expressed in and through local cultures, and reflecting the local context' (p. 135). This might mean, for liturgical legislators, that a greater variety must be allowed even in lectionaries and that alternative paths must be offered.

We have two lectionaries in use at present, those of the Prayer Book and the ASB, both with permitted variations. An Old Testament lesson has been provided for the Prayer Book eucharistic Lectionary and the readings for Morning and Evening Prayer come from modified 1961 Table of Lessons. ASB has additional readings for Ash Wednesday, Holy Week, Easter week, Ascension and Pentecost, and will soon have them for the period from Advent to Candlemas. Why should we not also have recommended or substitute readings for UPAs, for Communion with children, and for other types of parishes and groups? The fundamental lesson of liturgical history is that, for the early Church and the medieval Church, liturgical uniformity was unheard of. Not only were there different liturgical families of rites, each with its own distinct lectionary, but even within a given family, lectionaries did not always agree at all times and in all places. Churches used books that came from different periods and belonged to different types. Nowhere is there to be found a systematic attempt at organizing or reforming a system of readings. Neither Rome nor any of the great primatial sees tried to impose its choices on others. Perhaps the time has come for us also to accept such diversity and to reject the period of rigid uniformity and liturgical centralization as but one, perhaps misguided, phase of liturgical history and development. In part, this would be no more than a response to what is already happening. But it would require the provision of lists of suggested readings for a variety of occasions, such as those already provided in some of the new Roman Rites, together with a brief summary of content.

So what form of Calendar and Lectionary should the successor to *ASB 1980* provide? A new lectionary will inevitably be shaped by the two factors of tradition and contemporary need. The tradition pulls strongest in the celebration of the central mysteries of the faith and less strongly in the preparatory periods. Contemporary need, it seems, requires short, clear narratives that lead into the mysteries and allow them to permeate ordinary life. Anglican tradition pulls towards uniformity, even though this has already been effectively abandoned by allowing two schemes and their variants. Need points to a greater diversity even if it is contained within a general structure. These two factors can be met by a double structure.

First, in the seasons of Advent and Christmas and in Lent and Easter Lectionary and Calendar should be conservative. The central mysteries of the faith should be allowed to unfold in the way that tradition has demonstrated is most effective. In particular, Advent should recover its dominant eschatological dimension. And lections should be frequently used and re-used to provide a theological and liturgical foundation for Christian witness and a language for Christian conversation about the faith and its content.

Secondly, outside of these seasons it should be much more adventurous and innovative. Lectionaries do not have to be fixed for ever and contemporary need suggests a much greater emphasis on justice and peace, the option for the poor, solidarity with the oppressed, and the calling and mission of the whole people of God. A clear theological structure should be immediately evident. Themes should be boldly expressed and not merely given a brief and ambiguous title. The numerous special Sundays promoted by missionary and Bible societies and other organizations should be replaced by groups of Sundays exploring certain biblical themes, types and ideas in word and ritual. These series might follow Pentecost or Trinity and be structured like the Sundays after St Lawrence, Michaelmas, etc., noted above. By this means the liturgical proclamation would mirror and shape the concerns of the Church and material produced by central boards could be used for preaching, catechesis and for intercessions. As the ancient Roman liturgy expressed the concerns and history of that city, so the liturgy of the year 2000, courageously executed, could be truly inculturated, a bold statement of the faith of the Church of England proclaimed afresh to a new generation.

7

The Eucharistic Prayer

KENNETH STEVENSON

One of the points of difference between the ASB Rite A Eucharist and its sixteenth-century predecessor is that it contains four alternative forms of consecration, or 'eucharistic' prayer. For us who slipped with relative ease into the habit of using them, the ground had already been laid in 1970 when the Roman Missal of Paul VI appeared with its four eucharistic prayers. Indeed, if you look at most modern service books from the mainstream Churches, you are likely to find alternative provision at this point. It seems a sort of *Zeitgeist*, though, as the historians are quick to point out, to be in the position of having such a provision is not without precedent. The Byzantine rite has three, the Syrian Church has about seventy, and the old Visigothic rite of medieval Spain had numerous alternative sections of its eucharistic prayer.[1]

But now that we have used the ASB prayers for a bit and have had the chance of comparing them with what other Churches have at their disposal, it is hard to avoid some searching questions about what the next step for us might be. I offer here seven basic points of critique. I do so, not as a sort of liturgiological carper, but as a loving observer who thinks that while it is good that we have got as far as we have, we need to apply yet more energy if we are to arrive safely at the next stage.

First of all, *style*. The Church of England was late in joining the other Western Churches in the business of producing alternative anaphoras. This is shown by looking at what we have. There is something inherently unsatisfactory in being able to use two prayers (1 and 2) that are to all intents and purposes

43

the same, and two others (3 and 4) that arrived on the scene as a result of careful last-minute negotiation between Catholics and Evangelicals. In style, 1 and 2 are identical; 3 follows on as a recognizable cousin; but 4 is much more wedded to the Prayer Book approach, with its own particular theological concerns.

1 and 2 could profitably be amalgamated into one prayer that could be used in different ways, for example with the Prefaces extended in scope, and the possibility of using it as 2, namely with provision for the omission of virtually everything except the Proper Preface itself. 3 could be touched up, so that its inherent qualities could stand out more, such as the bold and traditional clause, 'he stretched out his arms on the cross'. Some new prayers could be written that don't say the same things in such a mannered way. We want, now, some *variety* in style.

Secondly, *language*. Among the criticisms of the ASB is the common complaint that it tends to use too much abstract language, and at a time when that language is not actually spoken by anyone, except by famous actors on television impersonating the caricature civil servant! I once attended a Eucharist for those with hearing and speech difficulties. Here, I observed the great problems which the person responsible for 'signing' the liturgy was faced with in some of the most central parts of the eucharistic prayer. In an age which is becoming increasingly conscious of children, of non-literacy in society, of the mentally handicapped, as well as the anti-intellectual climate of many higher educational institutions, it seems disingenuous that, for example, anaphoras persist in invariably referring to Jesus' 'death and resurrection', when 'dying and rising' are far more pungent, epigrammatic, resonant, and powerful.[2] There is an increasing desire for language that is more pictorial. Although many liturgical purists criticize the first post-communion prayer, the fact remains that it is manifestly popular. Its popularity lies largely in the fact that it tells a story: 'Father of all, we give you thanks and praise, that when we were still far off you met us in your Son and brought us home . . .'

Thirdly, *participation in the prayer*. The traditional answer to this question is that the prayer is that of the whole Church, and that the dialogue at the beginning is the means of bringing the congregation into what some of us call 'the eucharistic action'. But for some people this is just not enough. The prayer is often recited like a priestly monologue — an impression exacerbated by a tone of voice that is more reminiscent of a shopping-list approach to the Eucharist in general and the mighty acts of God in particular. In prayer 1, the congregation joins in with the doxology at the end; surely this provision should be built into the other prayers also. Often the other three prayers fall flat with a bald 'Amen'. In all the prayers, another type of acclamation is directed between the institution narrative and the anamnesis. There were arguments about the appropriateness of this development, not least because it divides two parts of the prayer that would appear to belong together. The *Lent, Holy Week, Easter* book permits other acclamations at this point, inspired by Roman Catholic flexibility.

But this somewhat wooden provision is not entirely satisfactory. There are occasions when they appear to come a bit reluctantly, such as a quiet weekday celebration. On the other hand, there are occasions, such as at a large Sunday gathering, when they do not seem to go far enough. Certainly, there is an argument for some sort of 'cue', particularly if the narrative and the acclamation are both going to vary.

One solution is to make the prayer more obviously participatory, to the point that it is written for responsorial recitation. There are good examples in some modern Anglican service books. But it needs careful compilation and regularity of use, otherwise the congregation is likely to be lost in its libretto. The best arrangement here is to use a repeated doxological response (e.g. 'To you be glory and praise for ever') at certain fixed points in the prayer. When set to music, the effect is even more powerful, which serves to underline the doxological nature of the eucharistic prayer. Some of the pressures towards this kind of involvement, however, come from congregations where it is thought successful to have as much noise and restlessness as possible, backed up, perhaps, by a sub-culture that is aggressively egalitarian in its style. Such a tendency can result in a eucharistic assembly in which everyone is vying for their corner — and worship goes by default!

Fourthly, the *seasonal character* of the prayer tends, at times, to fall limp, especially when the anaphora goes through the whole *curriculum vitae* of Christ, and then pinpoints a particular feature, sometimes (except in 2, when the CV can be omitted) as an afterthought. The Roman and Canadian Anglican books tackle this issue far more successfully, with an elaborate series of Prefaces which manage to hold together the (variable) seasonal element with the (total) general history of salvation.

Another way round this problem is to adopt a fresh approach to variety within the anaphora. People do not know the Bible as well as they once did and modern Christians are being introduced, or re-introduced, to the Old Testament at the Eucharist. Perhaps the eucharistic prayer ought to have a standard form, in the traditional 'salvation history' structure, but provision should be made for insertions at the Old Testament and New Testament stages. For example, a prayer on the resurrection might include the following insertions:

1. At the Old Testament: 'You delivered them from slavery and brought them to the promised land.'

2. At the New Testament: 'By his victory over the grave he burst the gates of death for ever.'

Such a model has been looked at by the Liturgical Commission. It meets the need for stability and the need for variety within one single prayer.

Fifthly, the *shape* of the ASB prayers,[3] as is well known, reflects the 'Alexandrian' pattern, which is taken as the norm for the Roman Catholic prayers also. Such a shape has the advantage of a particular pedigree within the whole Christian tradition, one which sees the institution narrative as, in some sense, predominantly 'consecratory'.

The other traditional shape for the eucharistic prayer (commonly called 'Antiochene') has only one epiclesis of the Holy Spirit, *after* the narrative and the anamnesis. This pattern was first adopted in Anglicanism in the 1764 Scottish Liturgy, but it soon spread to the USA, and it is known today all over the Anglican Communion. American Methodists also use it, and it is found in the Roman Catholic Church through ICEL's version of the anaphora of Basil of Caesarea.[4]

There are strong arguments for adopting such a shape in alternative anaphoras that are to be written for the coming decade. To invoke the Spirit on the gifts and the communicants at one and the same time seems to point to a more wholesome eucharistic piety. If the Spirit's task is to fulfil the intentions of the community as it celebrates the Eucharist, then that intention, surely, is to communicate faithfully in the Body and Blood of Christ. Another reason is that future anaphoras are likely to be shorter than those which were produced in the 1960s and 1970s, since there are many voices clamouring for less verbiage, more brevity. On that score, therefore, a shorter eucharistic prayer needs a less complex structure, and it would make better sense to keep both petitions for the Spirit to consecrate the elements and the communicants together. To deal with the Holy Spirit in one part of the prayer instead of two seems tidier, less repetitive, and more prudent. For those who are reluctant to detract from the centrality of the institution narrative, such a move in no sense undermines their position. The narrative character of the whole prayer serves to build up the story of the Supper to be of central importance, as the rationale for celebrating the Eucharist in the first place.

Such a move would also enable the principle of variety within the prayer, suggested earlier, to be extended, so that there might be alternative ways of praying for the blessing of the Spirit on the life of the Church. A variable epiclesis on the resurrection theme to match those quoted earlier might run as follows:

> Shine through the darkness of our doubt and sorrow,
> that the light of his risen presence
> may brighten the path before us.[5]

Some of the consecration language at the epiclesis in ASB might also be loosened up and made more vivid. The Greek liturgies at one stage used the verb 'to *show*'[6] as a way of speaking of the power of consecration. Such a rhetorical verb has the advantage of being strong without being mechanical, and personal without being wholly subjective.

Sixthly, the role of *Eucharist as offering*.[7] This aspect is insufficiently handled in the ASB prayers. It is well known that the words, 'we offer this bread and cup', were regarded as anathema by Evangelicals in 1966, and the subsequent discussions produced a truce that (on the one hand) insisted on the centrality of Calvary, and (on the other hand) leant on the concept of 'dynamic memorial' for the eucharistic action. (For the latter theme, see BEM and ARCIC statements.) But there is an argument for saying that the resulting text, particularly in prayer 1, produces a Zwinglian anamnesis, with an optional Catholic offertory rite. In other words, the bread and wine can be offered at the table before the prayer begins (or not, as the case may be), but the prayer itself must not have any sacrificial notions in it that may imply any hint of eucharistic sacrifice. This is a tricky area indeed, and it is one in which variety of treatment abounds from the earliest times, as has been shown by recent research. But the main criticism of the Catholic approach here has been, in the past, that it seems to make the Eucharist in some way 're-offer' Christ, a notion made explicit in the somewhat unfortunate wording of the Roman Catholic prayer IV ('we offer you his body and blood'). Protestants, however, can be equally strongly criticized for so nailing Christ firmly to the cross that he does not appear to be doing anything in the Eucharist. To 'immobilize Christ' is to do him, the Eucharist, and the Church a grave disservice.[8]

In the Church of England, there are several approaches to the issue of eucharistic sacrifice. There may well be conservative Evangelicals who are so extreme that they are Zwinglian in their understanding of the Eucharist, just as there may well be some Anglo-Catholics whose piety is positively medieval. But there are also many other shades of opinion. Some of us embrace the view of Calvin, with his strong emphasis on the high-priestly ministry of Christ in heaven. For them, the Eucharist is a 'pleading' of Christ's sacrifice. Others of us embrace the Reformed Patristic view espoused in the seventeenth and eighteenth centuries, in which the Church offers the gifts of bread and wine in remembrance of the one offering of Christ. For them, the Eucharist is a 'memorial-sacrifice'. Others again of us see the Lord's Supper in terms of the more radical 'Kingdom theology', in which the Church through the grace of the Spirit actualizes prophetic signs of Christ's kingship here and now. For them, the Eucharist is a meal of sacrificial solidarity with one another and the Lord. All three of these views are sensitive about any *exaggeration* of the uniqueness of Calvary so that Christ's priestly ministry in heaven is made 'immobile'; and they are also suspicious of 'offertory substitutes', whereby the ritual of presenting the gifts is, in some way, a sacrifice in its own right.[9]

Language that 'remembers' and 'celebrates' fails, at times, to make the vital link between what Christ is doing for us now and what we are doing in him at his table. To 'plead' Christ's sacrifice has a strong theological and hymnological pedigree, for the 'pleading' makes the link clear — and christological.[10] Moreover, in a eucharistic prayer where anamnesis leads straight into epiclesis, the 'pleading' takes on a yet more dynamic character, for we 'plead' the death of Christ, *so that* the Spirit may descend over the eucharistic table. In no way does this notion betray the Reformation; and it is a vivid verb still in regular use in other contexts in our overcrowded law-court schedules. An anamnesis and epiclesis might look something like this:

> Father, as we plead his sacrifice made once for all on the cross,
> we remember his dying and rising in glory,
> and we rejoice that he prays for us at your right hand:
> pour out your Holy Spirit over us
> and these gifts which we bring before you from your own creation;
> show them to be for us the Body and Blood of your dear Son.[11]

Finally, behind all this, there is the most fundamental message about the eucharistic prayer which liturgists have been trying to hammer home this century — that it is a *unity*. For most people, this comes home when a congregation has to decide what posture to adopt after the Sanctus. All the modern service books give strong hints that there should be no change of posture, so if you kneel for the eucharistic prayer, you should kneel throughout, and, equally, if you stand at all (as many do), you should stand for the entire prayer. And yet there are many places where the old piety persists. Layfolk up and down the country have a 'gut-reaction' that something sacred is about to begin after the Sanctus. Sometimes a compromise is reached and the old piety continues.

It is an interesting case in point. Many clergy collude with it, by dropping their voices from a 'proclaiming' tone to a 'mystic' one. Far better to keep to the same tone of voice throughout, but perhaps to drop the pace slightly at the institution narrative, since that is the psychological centre of the prayer. Far better also for people to stand throughout, but to learn to stand in silent adoration, in much the same way that many of our religious communities do as they celebrate the Eucharist.

But the unity of the prayer goes deeper still. If you fill the prayer with congregational responses, you risk disrupting the shape of the prayer. Moreover, if the responses are to be sung, then that is a strong argument for the whole prayer to be chanted, too. The internal unity of the eucharistic prayer is the heart of the eucharistic action. It tells the Christian story and asks God to realise it in a sacramental context. Even if the prayer has a tripartite structure (thanksgiving for mighty acts, supplication for the communion, and concluding doxology of Father, Son and Holy Spirit), the way in which each part flows on from the other is far more important than any manner of changes of voice, posture, or level of vocal participation.

Clearly these intricate linguistic, theological and aesthetic issues are not going to be resolved overnight. They are part of the nature of the eucharistic prayer. They are therefore worth paying attention to, so that we can give thanks in yet richer and perhaps more vivid and succinct ways than we do at present. Every new possibility creates fresh paths that the next generation can follow. In our particular age, we have had to try to bring to birth a new style of liturgical language as well. To achieve all of that in a short space of time is — as we have found — a tall order. But the instinct to worship eucharistically is far too deep in the soul of Christians for them not to reach out for something better when the chance is within their reach.

NOTES

1 See Kenneth W. Stevenson, *Eucharist and Offering*, New York, Pueblo 1986, for a discussion of this issue.

2 See Kenneth W. Stevenson, 'Lex Orandi and Lex Credendi — Strange Bedfellows?: Some Reflections on Worship and Doctrine', *Scottish Journal of Theology* 39.2 (1986), esp. pp. 235ff.

3 For a discussion of the history and development of this issue, see John H. MacKenna, *Eucharist and Holy Spirit*, Alcuin Club Collections 57, Great Wakering, Mayhew McCrimmon 1975. The writer is a Roman Catholic who comes out on the side of the 'Antiochene' shape.

4 For American United Methodist use, see *At The Lord's Table: A Communion Service Book for Use by the Minister*, Supplemental Worship Resources 9, Nashville, TN, Abingdon 1981. For the new Roman Catholic text, see *Eucharistic Prayer of Saint Basil: Text for Consultation*, Washington, International Commission on English in the Liturgy 1985.

5 Text drafted for the Church of England Liturgical Commission. The imagery is meant to be paschal, in the true sense of that word.

6 The classic example is in the Alexandrian anaphora of Basil of Caesarea, still used by the Coptic Church. For the Greek text, see A. Hänggi, I. Pahl, eds, *Prex Eucharistica*, Spicilegium Friburgense 12, Fribourg, Presses Universitaires 1968, p. 352. Latin-minded translators seem reluctant to admit the true character of this verb '*anadeixai*' as 'show'.

7 See *Eucharist and Offering* for this whole section. See also Kenneth W. Stevenson, *Accept This Offering: the eucharist as sacrifice today*, London, SPCK 1989, a shortened, thematic version of the larger work.

8 This thorny matter is sensitively handled by Rowan Williams, *Eucharistic Sacrifice: The Roots of a Metaphor*, Grove Liturgical Study 31, Bramcote, Grove Books 1982.

9 See Richard F. Buxton, *Eucharist and Institution Narrative,* Alcuin Club Collections 58, Great Wakering, Mayhew McCrimmon 1976, for a discussion of the way in which the 'offertory' came to be regarded as a substitute for eucharistic sacrifice in Anglicanism after the seventeenth century, pp. 110ff.

10 See Bryan D. Spinks, 'The Ascension and the Vicarious Humanity of Christ: The Christology and Soteriology Behind the Church of Scotland's Anamnesis and Epiclesis', forthcoming in T. J. Talley's *Festschrift*, to be published in 1989.

11 See above n. 5. See also Stevenson, *Accept This Offering*, pp. 79ff.

8

The Funeral Liturgy

MICHAEL PERHAM

The ASB revision of the funeral rites was one of the least radical, especially if the Series 1 (1928) rite was taken as the basis of revision. Certainly there was a change in mood, but in terms of structure, and indeed of some of the major texts, there was simply the sort of tinkering required to modernize the language and reach an acceptable compromise on prayer for the dead. The change of mood, and this was a very positive gain, was in a more confident and joyful proclamation of the Church's Easter faith, and a consequent loss of the medieval gloom that the Prayer Book had retained. But still, from its opening, 'I am the resurrection and the life . . .', the 1980 rite had a Book of Common Prayer feel and shape about it.

Why is that proving unsatisfactory? There seem to me to be two fundamental reasons. Both represent a twentieth-century development, and therefore do not deny the validity of the Prayer Book style for previous generations, but only its suitability for our present situation.

The first of these is to do with the nature and composition of today's normal 'funeral community'. In the past (and this is, of course, an idealizing of the past!) the funeral community was a natural one. It was natural in the sense that the people who constituted it were people who knew one another from day to day. The family did not return from 'away'. They lived near one another and, on this occasion, were joined by friends who were also neighbours. They were a community before ever they came into the church for the funeral. There was, consequently, little need to bind them into a community on

53

arrival in the church. The liturgy could afford to proceed on the basis of that shared sense of community, rather than have to create it as it went along.

But it was a natural one also in the sense that there was a common faith and common religious observance. Even when some of the people did not go each week to *that* church, they did go to church. They were on familiar ground in the liturgy, and they were not without knowledge of the basic tenets of the Christian faith.

The old rites (and for this purpose *ASB 1980* belongs in the same 'family') assume that sort of community: Christian people of faith, at home in church, and constituting a natural community. But the truth is very different. Even the family will come from all over the country, and will not necessarily know each other very well. The friends will be equally widespread. The neighbours may not be there. There will be a wide range of religious attitudes represented, from the deeply Christian to the perplexed doubter. Even when the funeral is of a member of the local church community, there will be many present from outside that community who do not have its shared experience and expectations.

The liturgy has to take all this seriously and create, very quickly, a shared sense of belonging, a relationship with one another, and an atmosphere of worship. Of course it is much helped by the one piece of genuine common experience: shared grief in the loss of one who was known and loved. It is on that that the minister must build.

The second pressure for radical change is the development of our understanding of grief. We are more aware than our forebears of how the processes of mourning work, and therefore of how the funeral liturgy can minister to these. As part of that we are beginning to learn what harm we may be doing to ourselves in 'distancing' ourselves from death. In a sense, the handing over of funeral liturgy to a priest, when once its leadership was a matter for the head of the tribe or family, was a first stage. But, in our own day, death in hospital rather than at home, the majority of deaths without a death-bed scene with family present and prayers said, the decline of the custom of the body lying in the front room, the handing over of the task of bearing the body to its grave to professionals, rather than this being a last gesture of service by the men of the family, have all distanced us from death, made us fear it more, and deprived us of the chance to see and to do things that help us to work through our grief and come to terms with death and bereavement. All of that, put alongside our greater under-standing of the nature of mourning, calls for a liturgy that helps us to take the body seriously, gives us more to 'do', and compensates in some way for all that has been lost by this distancing. It also calls for a slight redress of the balance of joy and grief, to take more seriously in the words of the liturgy the sense of the solemn and the painful, which the language of judgement was able to carry. The Easter faith does indeed need to be proclaimed powerfully, but Christian mourners need to grieve as much as any others.

These two problems are concerned above all else with the mourners. Of course a Christian funeral is about other things as well. Yet, if its communication with the mourners is not right, it will not so easily succeed in its other aims, of securing the reverent disposal of the corpse, commending the deceased to God, and proclaiming the communion of saints, the forgiveness of sins and the life everlasting.

These are modern problems, and ancient funeral rites cannot be criticized for failing to recognize them. But there is one other weakness in our rites that has long been there and recognized, but for which a solution seems hard to find. This is in our theology of afterlife, and therefore our prayer for the dead. There is no space to trace here the long history of prayer for the departed, and objections raised to it,[1] but it remains a problem for the Church of England. The Doctrine Commission wrestled with it in 1971, and published a report[2] which represented a careful and balanced theological perspective, to which all parties on the Commission subscribed, but the actual texts it commended were weak, and bore all the marks of compromise and the lowest common denominator. The synodical process did further damage, so that what emerged in the ASB Funeral Services was that all prayer for the dead was to be optional, and therefore not in the main text, and that the prayers consigned to the appendix should conform to the tentative and bald style of the Doctrine Commission's drafts. Except for Evangelicals, this was the worst of all worlds. If it was right to consign all prayers for the dead to the appendix so that their use was seen to be quite optional, then there ought to have been an opportunity to include among them some of the traditional prayers for the departed that have commended themselves to members of our Church. The prayers that are provided at present have neither the theological nor literary power to carry the emotions of the mourners, and most clergy have to search elsewhere for adequate words.

A lot of water has flowed under the liturgical and synodical bridges in the last ten years or so, and it ought now to be possible to move on from the agreed compromise of the 1970s into something that, while still sensitive to Evangelical concerns, can express the language of our communion with the saints in a richer and more satisfying form. Especially if it is agreed that the prayer for the dead should always be optional, and that other sorts of prayer should be provided as alternatives at key moments in the funeral liturgy, it must be hoped both that new texts, that can carry the support of the vast majority, can be agreed and included, and also that some traditional texts familiar in the Catholic tradition (from the simple 'May the souls of the faithful . . .' to the haunting words of the Contakion, 'Give rest, O Christ, to thy servant . . .') may be given space.

There are four specific areas where rethinking will be needed within the main funeral liturgy (to say nothing of the subsidiary

56

rites for receiving, interment of ashes, etc., for which at present only the most outline provision is made). The first is this provision of richer liturgical texts conveying our fellowship with the departed, our solidarity with them in prayer, and our affectionate commending them into the Father's hands.

The second is the creation of a rite that draws the community together. This will mean structural change more than anything else, and probably more of the shape of the eucharistic synaxis, even when Holy Communion is not celebrated.[3] Certainly it is the 'feel' of eucharistic worship that needs to be captured, with a higher profile sense of presidency than at present to bind together and give security. Part of this community concern will probably be a greeting at the beginning, a form of bidding ('We have come here today to . . .') and the provision of corporate silence.

The third area will be to take more seriously the sense of grief and loss, and to minister to it. This will involve the replacement of the prayer at the beginning of the 1980 rite, which begins the liturgy on a note of confidence, with something that faces grief and sorrow much more directly, and only comes later to a congregational affirmation of the Christian faith. People need time to get to that point. It will also probably involve the inclusion of some prayers with a more solemn tone. Something for instance that asks God to forgive the sins of the departed comes naturally in the service. We are conscious always at funerals of the tendency to idealize the dead, and that is not healthy. Ministry to the bereaved will surely mean also the bringing into the rite of a blessing at the conclusion. Of all occasions this is the one when people most need to feel the hand of God upon them in healing and blessing, and it is unfortunate that it is at present missing from our rites.

There is finally the need to take the body seriously, and to say farewell to it with strong words and maybe some symbolic action by the mourners. In the Roman rite there is the sprinkling with water that makes explicit the relationship between baptism and the grave, a theological theme that, in any case, needs strengthening in our rite. Maybe we can take that on board. If not, is there some other sign we can use? Might the mourners each light a candle from the paschal candle and place it around the coffin, for instance? Or do we just build on the non-Christian customs that are increasing, such as the single rose thrown into the grave, to fulfil this need? By one means or another we must bring the people close to the coffin and help them say 'Farewell' with words that have resonance and ritual that has meaning. At a funeral, of all services, the people must get up out of the pew and get involved.

NOTES

1 But I have written about this at some length in *The Communion of Saints*, London, SPCK 1980.
2 *Prayer and the Departed*, London, SPCK 1971.
3 Until 1552 the Eucharist was celebrated. It provided the 'communal celebration' that the burial office does not.

9

The Ambience of Liturgy

MARTIN DUDLEY

Attending an ordination service in York Minster, that irascible critic of ASB Peter Mullen observed wryly, 'You would not think it beyond the wit of man, even Modern Liturgical Man, to conduct an ordination in that setting, a form of service not discontinuous with the wonder of the place.' Mr Mullen dislikes 'terse, liturgical daleks' who tell God what to do in the language of office memoranda, together with colourful congregations, the demise of Prayer Book monarchism, and the shared Peace, and so he disliked this particular service very much. His cry is not new and it is not reserved to conservative clergy. Former Royal Shakespeare Company director Peter Brook wrote this in 1968:

> In Coventry, a new cathedral has been built, according to the best recipe for achieving a noble result. Honest, sincere artists, 'the best', have been grouped together to make a civilized stab at celebrating God and Man and Culture and Life through a collective act. So there is a new building, fine ideas, beautiful glass-work — only the ritual is threadbare. Those Ancient and Modern hymns, charming perhaps in a little country church, those numbers on the wall, those dog-collars and the lessons — they are sadly inadequate here. The new place cries out for a new ceremony, but of course it is the new ceremony that should have come first — it is the ceremony in all its meanings that should have dictated the shape of the place, as it did when all the great mosques and cathedrals and temples were built.[1]

He did not stop with this criticism. He saw that rituals were needed, that even the remnants of bankrupt forms can stir the heart, but that we do not know how to celebrate because we do not know what to celebrate. We have sometimes experienced the effective celebration. In a small group, bound together already by a common spiritual experience in retreat, we celebrated unity in faith and love, and found it meaningful. Or some occasion of true and unforced joy in one of the greater churches, soaring arches, endless processions, glorious singing, and the mysteriously exhilarating cadences of liturgical Latin or Tudor English. We know what it feels like and we long to find it again. We feel certain that one route or another will be the one that restores it: a friendly atmosphere, simplicity, freedom from set forms, lack of hierarchy, or a many-splendoured setting and all the traditional trappings of the holy drama. Yet oft repeated small-group worship proves unsatisfactory and unsatisfying and the day comes when *Light's abode, celestial Salem*, sung in solemn progress, loses its evocative power and neither a diet of novelties nor the Prayer Book lifts the troubled spirit. Something has gone wrong. ASB did not cause it and it has not proved to be a remedy for it and if many do find satisfaction in their Sunday liturgy it is in spite of rather than because of Rite A and its companions. So what is wrong?

It is not primarily the words. Rather it is that we are far too obsessed with getting the words right. That has been a limitation in several generations of English liturgists and it is a major one. The written text is paramount. Get that right and everything else will come right. But there is another text, the performed text, the true liturgical text, and that is as different from ASB as the performed play is from the study text. Rubrics have never been incidental to liturgy. But scholarly liturgists today seem still to be afraid that, in Dean Inge's memorable and unjustified phrase, they might be accused of being no better than butterfly collectors. In consequence 'ritualists', who often have a considerable knowledge of liturgy, are generally excluded from liturgical consultation. Yet, as Professor N. P. Williams, a leading Anglo-Catholic theologian, noted in 1933, 'ritualism' consolidated itself as a working religion 'conducting its worship with accompaniments of outward beauty calculated to enchain the emotions, and preaching a crisp and clear-cut system of doctrine easily apprehensible by the intellects of the poor and simple amongst whom its work lay.' Their ceremonial and their working theology came from the same source and served the same purpose, the salvation of souls.[2] Liturgy, pastoral care and evangelization need again to become partners in the celebration of Christ's saving work. And in this common venture the style and ethos of celebration is just as important as the text, the work of the ritualizer as vital as that of the scholar.

It is, after all, the *ordo* and not the bare text of prayers and propers that enables us to reconstruct medieval liturgies. You could not reconstruct much from ASB's 'blubrics'! Essential to the understanding of a play are the theatre, sets, actors, costumes, make-up, gestures, attitudes, accents, and all the dramatic panoply. In the same way, sacred space, ornaments, ministers, vestments, and the like are of the essence of liturgy. Without them, there is no liturgy, only words printed on a page. 'Liturgy', says Peter Mullen, 'is the theatre of the soul, but where are our modern liturgists?' Mostly they are studying old words or writing new ones! It could be argued that that is the safest approach to liturgy. W. H. Frere pointed out, in 1905, that 'the subject of religious ceremonial is one which has a special faculty for stirring strong feeling' and recommended prefacing any discussion of 'so dangerous a subject' with some general considerations 'calculated to minimise the dangers of explosion, to disarm prejudice, and to bespeak caution, patience, and charity.'[3] The dangers of strong feeling still exist but there is an increasing recognition that the liturgical totality is important and that the work of ritualization should continue or, rather, begin anew. This work is needed at every level and for every type of liturgical performance. To begin with we may need to follow Peter Brook's method and bracket out the words. The starting point is the reality of salvation. Liturgy is to be Christocentric. It is the saving work and its present reality that is being celebrated. The texts that express it should be interpreted visually, by gesture, movement, posture, ceremonial, and in works of art, however ephemeral. The meaning needs also to be expressed musically, both in the popular music of parochial liturgy and in more complex settings for choirs. Here it must be observed that some of the new responsorial texts prepared by the Liturgical Commission should offer unprecedented musical possibilities. Ritual action needs to be rediscovered as an expression of both faith and culture and this requires some careful thinking about the way in which we use signs and the material of signs.

The work of ritualization cannot take place in the study or in committee; it requires 'hands on' experience, experiment and imagination. The context of the work is the Christian community celebrating the dying and rising Saviour within the broad stream of liturgical tradition. That community is also a part of a culture or a number of cultures, and these and their expectations and desires should find a place in the ritual work. Theology is also a partner in this venture. The partnership involves two-way traffic. Liturgy is not simply to respond to movements in theology. The liturgy, text and action, is one of the sources of theology and the theologian must not reproach the imprecision of liturgical texts, their utilization of metaphoric forms, or the use of scriptural passages to convey a meaning which differs from the literal sense. The content of the liturgy is the same as that of Scripture, but it is presented in a different and frequently more powerful way. Liturgy precedes and does not presuppose Scripture. As Dom Prosper Guéranger observed, in the liturgy the Spirit who inspired the Scriptures still speaks to us. If we turn from the text to the whole and to the community which is the vehicle of celebration, we shall allow the Spirit to address us more directly.

This work, then, is not the responsibility of liturgical commissions or committees. It parallels their work. It is the work of the imagination and requires poets, artists, musicians, and dramatists, together with the new brand of interpreters of society whose study is semiotics, signs and signification. The liturgy must be truly inculturated. If the model for a new church architecture — which is yet to emerge — is the bringing together of traditional ecclesiastical forms and the contemporary vernacular architecture, so also the new ritual will emerge from a deliberate confrontation between classical liturgical form and the contemporary cultural values. But a service book in the year 2000 cannot be the immediate vehicle for that if we are thinking in terms of rubrics. Rubrics cannot overcome the dullness that is the dominant feature of so much liturgy and especially the powerful liturgies of confirmation, ordination and consecration which should be true celebrations of the faith community. So what are the options?

First, we could accept that it is impossible to legislate ritually and then the new book would include minimal statements about what is to be done and how. Most of the mandatory instructions could remain, as now, in the canons. Individuals or societies, like GROW, Alcuin, the Church Union, would be free to offer liturgical handbooks and ceremonial guides. Priests and parishes would be free to take up what they favoured. Diversity would flourish.

Secondly, we could preface the various rites with a theological and liturgical introduction in the manner of the revised Roman Rites. These would set out an official position and a typical form of each rite and require a certain adherence to it. Preparation of these preparatory statements would be a major task and would be beyond that which voluntary unpaid liturgists (which is what the Commission consists of) could be reasonably expected to do. That is not to say that it shouldn't be done but that it would require a greater seriousness in matters liturgical than the Church of England presently displays. And it would need a willingness to enforce liturgical law against all who violate it. So, despite the possible and considerable benefits, it would not be a popular option, but it might be the only way of raising standards of liturgical celebration.

Thirdly, we could continue and develop the present tendency of quasi-official commentaries and companions shaping the form and content of liturgical celebration. These are usually the private ventures of members of the Commission: liturgists commenting on the liturgies they have written! They could be supplemented by more official versions or by specific invitations to those who are not members of the Commission to contribute. Any such venture will be relatively conservative and there is little sign that it has improved liturgical standards so far.

The fourth method is less concrete and much less susceptible to episcopal or synodical control. The first thing that it requires is the relaxation of rules and a positive encouragement to experiment. But it also requires a willingness to submit to the mind of the Church, to allow the results of one's experiments to be critically received. In this method selected parishes and other places of worship are encouraged to perform a function akin to some medieval monasteries, especially Cluny and her daughters. They are to develop new liturgical forms and styles, to engage the Gospel dramatically with the world. At root this is an admission of ritual bankruptcy. What modern art has achieved, as for example in Salisbury Cathedral's 'Energy' frontal, modern ritual has not. There has been almost no advance since 1968. Unfortunately I think this is true. And if it is, then this work must be done before there can be a successor to the ASB and it would be very optimistic to plan it for AD 2000.

NOTES

1   *The Empty Space*, Harmondsworth, Penguin 1972, pp. 50-1.
2   *Northern Catholicism*, London 1933, p. 139.
3   *The Principles of Religious Ceremonial*, London 1905, p. 1.

10

The Language of Worship

MICHAEL PERHAM

It is part of the success of *ASB 1980* that there can be no real doubt that the main texts of any future service book will be in modern English, not unlike the style of the present book. This needs to be stated from the start, for all the shouting has come from the minority who resist that new style most strongly. But a silent majority has not just acquiesced in the change, but deepened its experience of worship through it. That is not something that one can prove, and it is something that some would challenge, but you would not find many parish clergy with thriving congregations who would say otherwise. The sheer success of the ASB, its sweeping introduction across the Church, far from being an episcopal plot, surprised bishops, Synod and publishers alike. The Church took to it like a duck to water. A series of essays that have examined its deficiencies needs to bear that in mind!

With the next round of revision, there will, however, be a fresh opportunity, and the first real chance since 1980, to 'carry' the 'Prayer Book people', to show them that their fears have been understood and their needs respected, and so to begin to reconcile and heal a Church where liturgy has been a source of discord. I do not believe that we can take everyone with us, for there are some for whom *any* alternative to the provision of the Book of Common Prayer is anathema, but I think there is a good chance that we can go into the next century less divided, and I believe that, in the search for the right way forward, we may find that we are enriching the liturgy for a much broader constituency. There are many more people who want to see Prayer Book material preserved and used in the liturgy than actually want to see a return to the pre-1967 days. There really are a great many 'not only . . . but also . . .' Anglicans when it comes to the language of worship, who want to go on being liturgically bilingual, or become more so.

They are not, on the whole, those who are wedded to the Book of Common Prayer for doctrinal reasons. They are not readers of *The English Churchman*, frightened that every new text brings us closer to Rome, and confident that every Prayer Book text used faithfully preserves us in the true Protestant faith of the Reformation. Nor are they those wedded to the Prayer Book because of the structure of its main rites. They may not know at all why the Prayer Book turns the traditional order of the Eucharist on its head. They wouldn't care too much if somebody altered the order of all the prayers round, providing they didn't tinker with the texts. Their devotion to the Prayer Book is therefore, at least in part, a literary matter. They know good English when they hear it, and they don't want it spoilt. But of course it goes deeper than that. Though for some it really is a matter of literature, or even of 'Englishness' (the culture lobby), for most it is to do with 'roots'. There is a marvellous sense of entering into a 'goodly heritage' about using the words, that not only you know by heart, but that your ancestors knew also. In a strange way it is about the communion of saints. That is not to be dismissed lightly.

Such people are selective about the texts they love and want to preserve. Most of them are the ones set to music, whether parts of the Eucharist, such as the Gloria, or parts of the office, like the Magnificat. This is not surprising, for most of us remember songs better than anything else, and the modern texts have been in general at their least satisfactory when set to music. The crucial texts also include, understandably, the Lord's Prayer and the Creeds. The latter, though sometimes set to music, have a different sort of status in people's minds, and tampering with them seems particularly outrageous. At one level it is of course right to argue that these texts did not begin life in fifteenth-century English, and that, if we really are interested in roots, we should dig right down to the early centuries and retranslate from Latin and Greek, but the fact is that it is in the language of the Prayer Book that these texts have come to us, and they have acquired the sanctity of the centuries. It is useless to point out the virtue of using the same translations that are used today across the continents, for the counter argument claims that that is no better than using today the translations used across the centuries. Who is to say which is the better argument? Perhaps it should also be added that almost the most beloved text of all is Cranmer's Prayer of Humble Access, and there is an important lesson about the fact that it is new composition, retained in the poetry of its original language, that people latch on to most.

This desire by a broad mass of people, not unsympathetic to liturgical revision, to retain certain key texts, is matched by the fact that, among those most wedded to the old, it is the rewriting of precisely these texts that irritates and annoys. People do not, in general, complain about the provision of 'The Song of Christ's Glory' as an alternative to the Nunc Dimittis at Evening Prayer. What they do complain about is the rewriting of the Nunc Dimittis that they have always found straightforward and intelligible. Give them their Nunc Dimittis unaltered, and they would, most of them, happily use the Song of Christ's Glory on other occasions. Similarly (and this was where the Synod made a mistake in the days of Series 3) people can respond to the completely new alternative to the Prayer of Humble Access ('Most Merciful Lord, your love compels us to come in . . .') because it is not a rewrite of a familiar and loved prayer, but a new composition. Is it not significant that one of the most popular prayers in the ASB is David Frost's absolutely new creation, 'Father of all, we give

69

you thanks and praise . . .'? In general we can draw the conclusion that the least contentious material in the ASB has been that which is quite new, and the most unacceptable has been the redrafting of familiar traditional texts.

A word should be said here about the process since 1980. There has been, by general consent, a recognition that in its natural desire to create a new liturgical style, less florid than that of the fifteenth and sixteenth centuries, and more in keeping with the spirit of the age, the ASB was at points almost too terse, direct and peremptory, though for some its very directness has been a great liberation. In *Lent, Holy Week, Easter* the Liturgical Commission tried to introduce a greater richness of imagery, and, as Kenneth Stevenson has written, that is continuing in the work of the present Commission. But it must take time for such a style to emerge and, meanwhile, there is no way to get it right except to go on composing and using. The best will survive and become part of the spirituality of the Church, like Cranmer's Prayer of Humble Access.

If we look back at the process of liturgical revision in the 1960s and 1970s it can be seen that it proceeded on the basis of a need to provide a uniformity of language. A modern English rite must provide a modern text for every prayer. Not a 'Thee' or a 'Thy' must remain. This sort of radical approach was probably both right and inevitable at the time. Anything less drastic would not have allowed the new liturgy to make its impact. Those most devoted to the Prayer Book would have been as opposed to a kind of mixture of language, old and new, as the keenest reformer. They were seen as forms best kept apart. Revision in other parts of the Anglican Communion proceeded on much the same lines, with traditional and modern language rites existing alongside one another without cross-fertilization at least in terms of language.

It was probably the publication of *Hymns for Today's Church* that first caused some to think again. Through the years before we had been using happily enough hymns in a whole variety of literary styles, with 'Thee' and 'Thou' in close proximity to 'You' and 'Your' without any pain. Most of us, not all, squealed with horror when we saw what had been done to many ancient hymns brought thoroughly into line, linguistically and theologically. It made one want to defend the use both of ancient and of modern texts in one service and to affirm that this could be done effectively and with integrity. And once we had said it about hymnody, why not about the mainstream liturgical texts? Most of us can live with a mixture of styles in worship, providing it is done with sensitivity. The ASB has done little to encourage us to do this, though it allows it by rubric with musical texts. But where we have done it, many of us have been happily surprised. It is the approach that was chosen for the 1988 Lambeth Conference.

Of course it is important to say 'most of us'. There are Christians, and many of them, for whom this cannot be true. There are, for instance, those in some of our inner-city areas and elsewhere, for whom the language of the sixteenth and seventeenth centuries belongs to quite an alien, or at least unknown, culture. There are also others, who though they might appreciate Shakespeare, for instance, as literature, would find the introduction of Prayer Book language into worship very strange, simply because they are 'new Christians' who have found their way to faith outside the traditional Anglican structure. It is the idea of *introducing* that would be so odd for some. It would not be a matter of keeping alive, or drawing from the memory, it would be absolutely novel and very strange. For some it might be a quite marvellous discovery; for many others it would be a barrier to communication with the living God. We cannot define Anglicanism as the acceptance of a particular style of liturgical language.

Could it be that the way forward will be to print, at *many* points in the liturgy, parallel texts, such as are now to be used with the Lord's Prayer in ASB services? Wherever there is a

71

traditional text, genuine composition or translation from the era of the Prayer Books, or another text that came into being before the liturgical revolution of the 1960s, could that not stand alongside the modern version, so that congregations may use the traditional words at any point in the service with the text printed in front of them, rather than relegated to an appendix or authorized by a rubric?

Were we to follow this way forward, we could simply have one modern eucharistic rite to stand alongside the Book of Common Prayer. There would be no need for a Rite A and a Rite B. One rite would suffice, in two columns where there was traditional material to be retained, and in one column of contemporary English at the points where there were no historic texts. This would give us, for instance, Cranmer's 'We do not presume . . .' (unmodernized) in parallel with Frost's 'Most merciful Lord . . .'. It would give us the Peace without a traditional text, for there is no such text. As for the canon, could not the contemporary eucharistic prayers include the Sanctus in two columns, and could not the first of the eucharistic prayers in Rite B (unmodernized) be added to the collection of more contemporary eucharistic prayers? It would be quite possible to use such a rite without ever resorting to an ancient text, and that liberty should be preserved; but, equally, for those who wanted to, there would be the option to use ancient and much-loved material and still to feel one was using the mainstream liturgy of the Church.

Although it is in the Eucharist that the major gain can be seen, for it would bring together those who now worship with separate rites, the process would also apply, for instance, to the Offices. The majority of the ASB canticles, which have no Prayer Book parallel text, would continue as they are. But Benedictus, Magnificat, Nunc Dimittis and Te Deum would appear in parallel columns. The same approach could be used with the pastoral offices, though there one sees less call for the Prayer Book material, and, in the marriage service, for instance, the parallel columns might appear only for the vows themselves.

In this consideration of the language of liturgy, no word has been said of the inclusive language issue raised by the feminist movement in the Church; and yet that is an issue that might seem to place a question mark against all the assumptions of this essay. It is a major question, and so has been given a chapter of its own (which follows), but this has preceded it lest anyone think that the only language issue is one relating to the place of the feminine in the worship of the Church.

The kind of solution proposed here to the wider language question will not satisfy everybody. There are those who will not consider it, and there is almost a perversity in the attitude that will not touch a modern text lest it contaminate the pure old religion of the Prayer Book. But for many the abandonment of the principle of a single linguistic style for any particular service, and the acceptance that the best from across the centuries (including our own) can exist together, presents an attractive possibility of a cross-fertilization that has the power to reconcile.

The alternative seems to be the continuance of two churches, traditional and modern, within one parish. That division will mean that eventually, and in some cases within a generation, the traditional will die. There are some who see that as the natural end of the present liturgical reform. Others of us want to see the best of the Anglican liturgical tradition, including the texts of its ancient liturgy, taken on into the new century *and used*, but within a liturgy that is thoroughly contemporary and appropriate for the age.

Jesus did say something about the difficulty of putting new wine into old skins. But he also commended the householder who could produce from his store both the new and the old. It is just such a store that we need in the new liturgy of the Church.

11

Affirming the Feminine

MICHAEL PERHAM

Quite the most difficult essay that anyone could be asked to undertake in this collection is one about the place of the feminine in the liturgy of the Church, and in particular in liturgical texts. It is difficult because in no other area of theological and liturgical thinking has there been so much movement in a very short time, and because this changing scene looks set to continue at such a pace that to outline how it should be tackled in a book to be authorized in the year 2000 is all but impossible. Yet we must try.

In 1980 there was no widespread consciousness in the Church of England of a rejection by some women of the language of 'men', 'man' and 'brethren', nor was there any demand to say in the liturgy things about God that gave the feminine greater prominence. Yet within just two or three years some phrases were beginning to look, to some at least, strikingly inappropriate, none more so than the 'living in love and peace with all *men*' of Holy Communion Rite A. By 1986 there was a good deal of literature around to stimulate discussion, and the particular issue of how the Church of England should modify its language was being spelt out by Vivienne Faull and Jane Sinclair in *Count Us In — Inclusive Language in Liturgy.*[1] Soon after the Church of England Liturgical Commission was being asked for guidelines, and its recommendations are now available to the Church. Conservative as they are, they represent the latest stage in a movement that, as far as England is concerned, has come from nowhere to the centre of the liturgical stage in less than a decade.

However are we to know what will be right in ten years' time?

One thing that is becoming clear is that England is out of step with much of the Western English-speaking world. These issues were around in America in the 1970s, even if they were not so in England. In the 1980s the Anglican liturgies of several countries, notably the United States, Canada and New Zealand, have gone quite a long way in removing language that might be considered exclusively masculine. The latest texts proposed by the English Language Liturgical Consultation (ELLC) go further, and begin to tackle the maleness of our language about God and, in particular, the pronouns 'He' and 'Him' that most of us use quite unthinkingly. Protests against these developments, such as those by Professor David Frost in Australia, have gone largely unheeded, except here in England, where there is both a marked reluctance to take the matter seriously in some communities, and also a real antagonism to the inclusive language issue, sometimes from articulate educated professional women, in others.

If a decision had to be taken now, it is fairly certain that the Church of England would opt to break with ELLC, and agreed texts for the English-speaking world, rather than adopt translations that are seen as grave impoverishments linguistically and theologically. The majority feeling would be that changes had been made for a cause that had not yet proved it was here to stay. The recognition is growing that international texts are bound to come into conflict with a trend to take the *cultural* setting seriously. What is right for America may be wrong for England. And this may be true, though, of course, it involves an over-simplification. For England is itself a land of different cultures. In some of them questions about the role of women are pressing; in others no issue has been perceived.

The question of perception is important. For we are not agreed on whether liturgical change in this area should be in response to a perceived problem or whether it should help that problem to be perceived. In other words, do we change the words of the liturgy because people *find* them unhelpful, stifling or exclusive? Or do we change the words of the liturgy because they *are* exclusive, and people ought to be finding them so and realizing that they had been, all unconsciously, trapped in a view of things that was repressive, narrowing and exclusive?

Those who have argued most passionately for change have done so partly from their sense of hurt, and partly from their sense of truth. Both have to be taken seriously, though the second has far more radical implications.

The sense of hurt says simply: 'I find this language exclusive. When I hear the words of a liturgy where God is spoken of only in masculine terms, and the words "man" and "men" feature regularly, but "woman" and "women" hardly at all, my sense of dignity and value is undermined. I feel second rate and I feel excluded.' That is the sense of hurt, which is very real and genuine. It is not felt by all women. Indeed it sometimes seems that one hears more women pour scorn on it than men. But that doesn't alter the fact that it is felt by some women, and men also, and that that number of people seems to be increasing.

One can respond to that hurt by thinking it through and coming to the conclusion that these women are right. The language we use does undermine and devalue. But one can also respond by rejecting the argument, while recognizing that the hurt is genuine. In effect one is saying, 'I don't believe these words ought to give any one a sense of exclusion, but I recognize that you *do* feel excluded by them, and so I will try to use some other words that affirm you. I will talk about "brothers and sisters" (or even "sisters and brothers") rather than "brethren". I will speak of Christ becoming "human", rather than Christ becoming "man". I will do these things so that you may feel included, in a way I have never doubted you are included.'

It is at that level, the level of being sensitive to a perceived hurt, that many clergy and others have begun to modify the language of liturgy. And, in a way, it doesn't matter if there is only one person in a congregation of a hundred who feels this hurt. It still makes sense to modify the liturgy to 'count her in', providing nothing crucial is lost.

But the argument about truth is, of course, more fundamental. It is not simply a matter of good pastoral practice. For this argument says not so much 'I *feel* excluded' as 'Women *are* excluded'. If year by year, century after century, we talk about our God and about our human race in masculine terms, it makes no difference that we keep saying 'the masculine embraces the feminine'; we must be assimilating, at a subconscious level, a belief that somehow the male is primary, or normal, or superior. Through most of human history, the language we have used both of divinity and of humanity has put women down, subjugated them. Both men and women have been conditioned by it. We are all, men and women, the victims of this misrepresentation of the way God is and God meant the human race to be, and language has been a powerful tool of that misrepresentation. We have lost sight of the truth that 'male and female created he them', and both were in his image.

Now, if that argument holds up, it is infinitely more important than the argument from hurt, and it makes the case for reforming the language of liturgy to make it more inclusive, not when people demand that, but in order that they may no longer be misled by a language that has served them badly. Language, that has been a tool of their repression, must now be used as a tool of their liberation.

If we accept this argument, it matters not that people will protest — as they do — that they don't need to change the language because they do understand that the male includes the female. For they have missed the point. Why *should* the female be hidden within the male? Why should its inclusion be only a matter of implication? Is not every instance of 'the male includes the female' one more assertion of masculine dominance, from which men, as much as women, need to escape? There is an increasing number in the Church deeply impressed by this argument from truth, but the majority is not convinced. It remains difficult to see which changes of language represent a major shift in thinking and which a passing fad.

The recent Liturgical Commission recommendations[2] go only a small way down the path of making the liturgy more overtly inclusive. What they propose is for an interim, for the adaptation of *ASB 1980* by those who wish to. It does not face at all what should happen in 2000, though in its own current work it tries to follow its own moderate guidelines, and succeeds most of the time. The basis of its recommendations is that nothing is to be enforced, and the texts of *ASB 1980* remain in force, but where alterations are desired they may legitimately be made in line with a schedule it provides for each occasion in the ASB when 'exclusive' language is perceived. Not all the recommended alternatives have equal weight, and some would commend themselves to many people and others to only the most determined 'inclusivizers', but an alternative has nevertheless been provided in every case (except the Creed) so that those who wish to change all the texts may use the best variant the Commission can find. In each case the Commission looked at the word or phrase under discussion, and looked for the variant that was most satisfactory in terms of theology, literature and rhythm.

Through its approach it has tackled quite effectively the whole business of 'cumulative exclusion'. By this I mean that part of the problem for women is that the words of which they are suspicious *keep* appearing. 'Mankind', 'man' and 'men' are scattered liberally through the liturgy. Though there are some for whom it is important that *every* case be removed, for many the problem goes away if the incidence of these words is reduced considerably. Some would say, that if the vast majority of the instances of the use of these excluding words were removed, all the occasions when there is no theological or literary loss, they could live with the ones that remained, because there would no longer be a cumulative sense of exclusion. The Liturgical Commission believed, for instance, that there was an important theological loss in sacrificing 'For as by man came death by man came also the resurrection of the dead' in the Easter Anthems. Perhaps the verse would not offend if it were an isolated instance, rather than part of a general style.

But the Commission did not face the issue of *crucial* texts. Though many could live with the retention of male imagery at a limited number of points, where some important meaning required its retention, they could not live with it at the points of deepest significance in the liturgy. In the Roman Church this has focused chiefly on the eucharistic prayer with its 'given for you and for all men'. In the Anglican rites this is avoided, but the focus is on the Creed. The Creed, of all liturgical texts, is the one where you want your deepest aspirations affirmed. 'And was made man', for some, simply will not do! While that is retained, without alternative, there can be no satisfaction for those seeking an inclusive liturgy. The justification for making no change now is that it would be too serious an alteration to be made without full synodical approval. It could not be done under the canons. Before 2000 it will have to be faced.

The report also points to what the Commission believes is the better way to affirm the feminine than tinkering with existing texts. Better, it argues, to use what we have, with all its male bias, but put alongside it new material that affirms the feminine. Better to affirm both masculine and feminine than to opt for a kind of genderless lowest common denominator. This is an attractive line, and it is probably in this area that most work now needs to be done. But it is much more difficult than people imagine, and the paucity of the material the Commission includes indicates the problem. A handful of canticles, a collect or two, and not much more, receive the *imprimatur*. It hardly begins to redress the balance and celebrate the feminine.

What are the problems in undertaking this sort of creative writing and editing?

The first is the lack of texts in the Scriptures and in the tradition. Some important questions about biblical authority are being raised if, in order to find scriptural sources, you are forced to look almost exclusively in the Apocrypha! The Wisdom literature is the best source, but the material is, frankly, obscure, and would not find its way into the mainstream liturgy except as a rather desperate scraping of the barrel to find the feminine affirmed. But doesn't that show just how deep the problem is? It is not so much our liturgy that is irredeemably masculine, but our biblical revelation. It is our theologians, rather than our liturgists, who have to tackle that.

The centuries of tradition do not much help. Of course everybody knows that Mother Julian wrote very movingly about Jesus as our mother, but she was a great exception (the Liturgical Commission finds another in St Anselm, though probably not Anselm at his most typical), and what she wrote is desperately difficult to turn into a liturgical text. Once again we are forced to the view that texts that affirm the feminine will have to be new ones, without much Scripture or tradition even as source. Is the Church willing to sanction that sort of creativity, or, at least, prepared to place the results of it in its service books?

Another problem is that where, rather clutching straws, material can be drawn from Scripture or tradition, it is almost entirely about motherhood, labour pains, breasts and milk. And, indeed, much of the more creative writing from the 'women's movement' in the Church, even without Scripture and tradition in mind, relies heavily on these images. There is an irony about this, which I suspect women have not yet entirely faced. The women's movement in society has been in part a liberation of women from the role of mother, a recognition that for her fulfilment a woman may need to pursue a quite different path, may opt not to be a child-bearer, and to escape from domesticity. Yet, when it comes to liturgy, it is child-bearing, breast-feeding, and labour pains that, time and time again, are used to affirm womanhood in worship. That is an unresolved contradiction with which we have to wrestle.

There is a further problem about writing new texts. It is in the *depersonalizing* of God. The Holy Spirit has nearly always been the least easy person of the Trinity to which to relate, simply because you don't bump into holy spirits in ordinary life in the way you do fathers and sons. God is real for us because we all know what fathers are like and what sons are like. We are less sure about holy spirits. Some within the Christian feminist movement, in an attempt to free God of maleness, and yet not to saddle him/her with a femaleness that would be equally exclusive, prefer a Trinity of Creator, Redeemer and Sanctifier. That is perfectly orthodox, and, at one level, cannot be criticized, but, at another level, it is a description that is almost bound to make God remote. For we do not meet creators and redeemers like we do fathers or sons, or even mothers and daughters. We do not immediately respond to the image, nor would it encourage us into a relationship. This is but one example of a tendency to make less personal and more remote by avoiding, simply because they are divided by gender, the nouns and pronouns we associate with human beings. This is a theological impoverishment that needs to be taken with the utmost seriousness. To be fair, many who are seeking a non-inclusive language do recognize the problem entirely.

The contributors to this book represent a fairly typical wide range of attitudes to inclusive language, and as such simply reflect the diversity of opinion in the Church, both among men and women. This essay has been written by one who is convinced that there is a case for a thorough rethinking of the

82

liturgy to affirm and celebrate the feminine. I do think it is a matter of 'truth' as well as of 'hurt', and I see myself as a friend of the feminist movement. But I do not believe that some very difficult questions have been faced by the 'inclusivizers' any more than by those who see no problem with our present use of language, and I do not believe these liturgical questions can be faced very effectively until the prior theological issues have been tackled boldly. Nothing less than our doctrine of God is at stake.

NOTES
1 Bramcote, Grove Books 1986.
2 *Making Women Visible*, London, Church House Publishing 1989.

12

The Processes of
Revision and Authorization

DEREK PATTINSON

Law and Practice

Worship in the Church of England is regulated by the provisions of the Church of England (Worship and Doctrine) Measure 1974, and by Canons made under its authority. The Measure provides that the forms of service in The Book of Common Prayer of 1662 shall 'continue to be available for use in the Church of England'. Apart from that condition, the Measure and the Canons give to the General Synod the right to approve forms of service for use in the Church of England, to amend forms of service which it has itself approved, and to continue or discontinue such services if it (the Synod) thinks fit. These powers extend to the provision (or amendment) of collects, tables of lessons and rules for ordering services. The Measure requires, however, that in exercising these powers the Synod's decisions are not to have effect unless, when a decision is finally approved, there is a majority in each of the three Houses of the Synod — Bishops, Clergy and Laity — of not less than two-thirds of those present and voting.

In addition to the provisions thus made for the continuance in authorization of the Book of Common Prayer 1662, and for services to be approved by the General Synod, the Measure and Canons — in particular Canon B1 — also continues the authorization of the shortened forms of Morning and Evening Prayer 'which were set out in the Schedule to the Act of Uniformity Amendment Act 1872': in effect, the 1662 forms of those services as commonly and customarily used in the Church. Furthermore, the 1974 Measure and Canons also safeguard the powers of the Crown, by Royal Warrant, to authorize forms of service for use on the anniversary of the Accession and to change the names of the Sovereign and other members of the Royal Family used in authorized services of the Church of England and any other 'necessary alterations'.

Finally, the 1974 Measure and Canons give powers to the Convocations, the Archbishops or the Ordinary to authorize forms of service 'for use on certain occasions'. In effect, a Convocation may provide a form of service for use in its province on an occasion for which no provision is made in the Book of Common Prayer or by the General Synod; the Archbishop may authorize a form of service for use in his province if no provision has been made in the BCP, by the General Synod or by his Convocation; and the Ordinary — in a parish church, the parish priest — may authorize a form of service where no provision has been made by the other authorities.

The General Synod's aim in the 1974 Measure and the associated Canons was to make comprehensive provision for the future handling by the Church of England, or on its behalf, of its liturgical business, and, as part of the same powers, to repeat the Acts and Measures which had previously been in force. Everything, even the 1662 Book of Common Prayer, now derives its statutory authority ultimately from the 1974 Measure.

It is, however, necessary, to look at the situation prior to the coming into effect of the 1974 legislation, to identify and understand the various elements incorporated within that legislation and the relationship between them.

The Prayer Book of 1662 was originally authorized by the Act of Uniformity 1662, to which it was annexed as a Schedule. It followed from this that the replacement of the 1662 Book by some other Book, or the amendment of the 1662 Book, or of the parent Act, could only be achieved through Parliamentary legislation. In the event, the main text of the 1662 Book remained, and remains, virtually unaltered. There were, however, Acts of Parliament from 1871 onwards which gave authority for the more flexible use of the Prayer Book and for the substitution in 1871 and 1922 of new lectionaries.

After the revival of the Convocations in the latter part of the nineteenth century there was much pressure for Prayer Book revision. Little progress was made until the Enabling Act 1919 gave to the Church Assembly delegated powers from Parliament to enable it to legislate by Measure on *any* matter affecting the Church of England, subject to the requirement that a draft Measure, when finally approved by the Assembly, would be submitted to the two Houses of Parliament, for consideration in each House on an affirmative resolution. If the two Houses responded in the affirmative, then the Measure went forward for the Royal Assent exactly like an Act of Parliament. The Church Assembly, not surprisingly, decided to try to use the new procedure as a vehicle for securing the authorization of a revised Prayer Book. The Assembly went twice with proposals to Parliament. In 1927 a Measure authorizing a revised Book was approved in the House of Lords, but rejected by the House of Commons. In 1928 the Church Assembly tried again, having modified the text of its revised Book in an attempt to meet the Commons' criticisms. Again, the proposal was approved by the Lords but rejected by the Commons.

In the wake of the failures of 1927 and 1928, it could be, and was, argued by legalists of an Erastian persuasion that the only forms of service which were duly and lawfully authorized for use in the Church of England were those contained in the 1662 Book, subject only to such (relatively) minor modifications as had been allowed by nineteenth- and twentieth-century legislation or by Royal Warrant. But the archbishops and bishops, for their part, let it be known that they would consider it proper in the circumstances to use in public worship any of the additions and deviations which the 1928 Book would have allowed. By this act, the archbishops and bishops effectively claimed — whether intentionally or not — an 'authority' in matters liturgical which in some sense and to some extent paralleled or qualified that of Parliament. Meanwhile, the revived Convocations in their respective provinces and the archbishops and bishops in their dioceses had been authorizing forms of service to meet the developing needs of the Church for occasions and circumstances for which no provision was made in the 1662 Book, e.g. forms of service for use at the institution and induction of an incumbent and at the dedication or consecration of a church. At the same time, incumbents (encouraged by the bishops to draw on material from the 1928 Book) had already in many instances also been drawing freely, when conducting services, including statutory (Prayer Book) services, from non-Prayer Book material. In some instances, indeed, this tendency went to the point when substantially the forms of service used contained hardly any Prayer Book material. Most bishops tried to hold their clergy to 1662 and 1928 material. Whether or not they took action where clergy went beyond these bounds varied from diocese to diocese and from bishop to bishop. Some people — bishops, clergy and laity alike — were content 'to let things drift', at least until it became possible to take up again the cause of Prayer Book revision. Others, however, felt that the action of the Convocations and the bishops in relation to the authorizing of services — whether 1928 services or non-statutory services — and, indeed, the action of the incumbent, as ordinary, could be justified by appeal to a *ius liturgicum*, a somewhat shadowy concept which they discerned behind and above the actions of Parliament in enacting the Act of Uniformity, and to which appeal might properly be made in the wake of Parliament's refusal, in the face of the Church's expressed wish, to authorize a revised Prayer Book.

When, forty years later, there could be a fresh attempt at

liturgical revision, it was clear that account would have to be taken not merely of what was 'lawful' in the narrow Erastian sense (i.e. the 1662 Book) but also of the main thrust of what had been allowed to flourish side by side with that Book. Under the Prayer Book (Alternative and Other Services) Measure 1965, the Convocations and the House of Laity of the Church Assembly were given temporary powers (to expire in 1980) to authorize services alternative to those in the 1662 Book — the aim being (at least at the outset) to arrive by 1980 at a generally acceptable revision of the Prayer Book. As a first step the bishops proposed that the main variants which the Church had come to use, post 1928, should be brought within the lawful pale. To achieve this, they arranged for the preparation of texts of the statutory forms of service *as they had come to be used*, incorporating some 1928 material but not all — and some other material. These forms of service — the Series One Services — were approved by the Convocations and the House of Laity under the 1965 Measure. The traditional additions and deviations thus became as 'lawful' as the 1662 Book.

When the 1965 Measure, with its temporary provisions, was replaced by the 1974 Measure and Canons (which gave the Church permanent powers), the new legislation covered all the bodies which had come to exercise authority in liturgical matters in the Church of England — the Crown (by Royal Warrant); Parliament; the General Synod (inheriting the powers of the Convocations and the House of Laity); the Convocations; the Archbishops; the Bishops; the Ordinary; and, finally, the right of the minister in any service to make minor departures from prescribed forms. All these bodies now derive their legal authority from the provisions of the Measure, and not from any earlier or other authority: the *ius liturgicum*, if and to the extent that it existed, can no longer legally or morally be prayed in aid.

When in 1965 and 1974 Parliament agreed to give to the

Church powers in matters of liturgy which it had previously exercised itself, two principal conditions were built into the legislation. First, both in 1965 and in 1974, power was given to bodies with a comparatively large membership and which included a substantial lay element. Under the present (1974) arrangements, bishops, clergy and lay people generally meet together for debate. But, following the practice settled in 1965, they vote separately and two-thirds majorities are still required in each House. All this reflects a continuing concern in Parliament that the powers should not fall into the hands of a small caucus, whether episcopal or clerical, and that new services should only be authorized if there was clear evidence of a wide, general, acceptance of them, to which the synodical voting would bear witness. But if Parliament was concerned about this matter, so were many on the Church side, most particularly the members of the House of Laity.

The second condition, introduced for the first time in the 1974 legislation, related to the 1662 Book of Common Prayer. Between 1965 (when the Prayer Book (Alternative and Other Services) Measure took effect) and 1974 the thrust of liturgical revision had changed. It became clear that a book completely to replace the 1662 Book was unlikely to be a realistic aim: either it would retain too much of the 1662 material to satisfy those who wished to see major change or it would abandon so much of the traditional material (and language) to be unacceptable to the more cautious.

The 1974 legislation was based on the recommendations of the Archbishops' Commission on Church and State (1970). While recommending that the General Synod should have permanent powers in the field of liturgy, the Commission was divided on the issue whether these should include a power for the Synod itself, at some future date, to order the discontinuance of the liturgical use of the 1662 forms of service, or of particular items among them. The matter was put to the Synod: its decision was that the projected Measure giving permanent powers should 'entrench' the 1662 Book, and it so provides. Thus, if the Synod should ever wish to withdraw the authorization of the use of any Prayer Book service it would have to legislate by Measure (and thus secure Parliamentary approval).

The Course of Liturgical Revision 1965–80

As already indicated, the first use of the 1965 'temporary' powers was to authorize the Series One forms of service. Once these services had been approved, the Convocations and the House of Laity went on to consider a second series of alternative services — alternative to the Prayer Book and Series One services. Like them, they were worded in traditional language. But in their content and shape they were 'new', reflecting the results of the liturgical scholarship of their day and taking account of perceived pastoral needs. This range of Series Two services was never completed, partly because of disagreements over particular forms, e.g. the proposed Series Two forms of services for funerals and for marriages, and partly because of an increasing pressure that there should be a series of alternative series in modern language. In 1973 the General Synod, which had by then inherited the (temporary) powers of the Convocations and the House of Laity, authorized Holy Communion: Series Three.

The replacement of the temporary powers given in 1965 by the Church of England (Worship and Doctrine) Measure 1974 opened the way to a reformulation of the Church's aims in the programme of liturgical worship revision in which it had engaged. It was settled in 1974–5 that the Church should aim, by 1980, to have authorized and available an Alternative Service Book which (as its title suggested) would contain an alternative to each of the main forms in the Book of Common Prayer. It was agreed, too, that ASB services should be — with one exception — in modern language. It was also settled that the General Synod would, between 1974 and 1980, approve a full range of Series Three services, it being understood that, once approved, these would be included in the 1980 Book, with no further amendments apart from editorial tidying-up. To these general understandings, there were two major qualifications. It was agreed that, exceptionally, the Series Three Holy Communion Service (1973), the first Series Three service, should be the subject of a major revision before being included in the ASB. Hence it is the revised, and not the original, Series Three modern language Communion rite which appears (as Rite A) in *ASB 1980*. Secondly, it was agreed at a comparatively late stage to include, amongst what for the rest was material in modern language, an alternative traditional language Communion rite (Rite B), derived from a combination of the Series One and Series Two Communion rites.

The *ASB 1980* was published on schedule in the closing months of 1980. As well as authorizing the services within it, the General Synod continued, initially for five years, some of the Series One material, some Series Two material and the original Series Three Communion rite.

Developments after 1980

In effect, between 1980 and 1985 parishes could choose between BCP, ASB and the surviving 'Series' material. In each case there was choice between BCP and alternatives to it in traditional and in modern language. In 1985 the General Synod narrowed the range of choice so that, of the Series material, only Series One Matrimony and Burial services and Series Two Baptism and Confirmation services remain in formal authorization. While the Synod in 1985 showed itself ready to narrow the range of authorized material, there was nevertheless pressure from some church people to restore the authorization of the Series One services of Baptism and Holy Communion. The House of Bishops had some sympathy with these aspirations. It became clear, however, that the Synod would not be prepared formally to re-authorize these services under the alternative services procedure. In 1988, however, the House of Bishops resolved the problem by registering the opinion that the use liturgically of material which had at any time since 1965 been authorized for use and was well established in local usage, even if no longer formally authorized, would be regarded by them as within Canon B5(1) as a variation 'not of substantial importance'.

Since 1980 the Synod has made only one addition to the body of services formally authorized, as the services in ASB 1980 are authorized, under the 1974 Measure and Canon namely, in 1983, in respect of the Ministry to the Sick. The full authorization procedure had to be used in respect of these services since they are alternatives to services within BCP. In 1985–6 the General Synod formally extended the period of authorization of the *ASB 1980* and the Ministry to the Sick 1983 to 31 December 2000.

As a development from the practice of formal synodical authorization, preceded as it must be by careful scrutiny of draft services in the Synod, the House of Bishops has developed the practice of 'commending' forms of service for use in the Church. The process of commendation cannot be used in respect of services which are alternative to BCP services. It can, however, be used in respect of other liturgical material. If a form of service is 'commended', it is for the individual diocesan bishop to authorize its use in his diocese. The first examples of the new process are the Services of Prayer and Dedication after a Civil Marriage (1985) and the volume of services, etc. for use in Lent, Holy Week and Easter (1986). In these cases the texts were circulated to the Synod. There was no formal process of synodical scrutiny and amendment, but comments were invited from Synod members and others interested. These comments were then considered by the Bishops, with the advice of the Liturgical Commission. The final text was settled by the House of Bishops alone, with no further involvement of the Houses of Clergy and Laity.

Preparation of draft services, etc. for approval or commendation: the present practice

Under the 1974 Measure and Canons and the relevant Standing Orders of the General Synod, it generally falls to the Liturgical Commission to prepare, for consideration by the House of Bishops, the first draft of any form of service (or other liturgical text) which the Synod is then to be asked to authorize, or which the Bishops are to consider for commendation to the Church. There are occasional exceptions, e.g. work now proceeds on a new Catechism, where the Board of Education is taking the lead on the bishops' behalf, though the Liturgical Commission and the Doctrine Commission are represented on the drafting group.

There has been a Liturgical Commission since the late 1950s. Since 1971 it has been appointed by the Archbishops in consultation with the General Synod Standing Committee. Its formal terms of reference give it three responsibilities — to prepare draft forms of services for submission in the first instance to the House of Bishops; to advise on the experimental use of forms of service so approved; and to be a clearing house for the exchange of information and advice on liturgical matters with other Anglican provinces and other Churches.

When the present Commission was in process of appointment (1985–6) the Standing Committee of the Synod published a report, *The Worship of the Church* (GS 698). The Standing Committee's Policy Sub-Committee had itself prepared the report, in consultation with members of the outgoing Commission and others; and before the document was finalized it was considered at a separate meeting of the House of Bishops. In effect, it amplified the basic terms of reference of the Commission by suggesting the outline of a programme of work for the present Commission (1985–90) and thereafter. It was at this point that the Synod agreed to the extension of authorization of *ASB 1980* to the year 2000, thereby effectively deferring until the next decade any major revision of the 1980 Book.

The procedure for the preparation of draft services and for their approval by the Synod is, essentially, that which was developed in the 1960s and 1970s, and of which *ASB 1980* was the eventual outcome, though standing orders were modified in 1986 in the light of experience gained then. When the Commission is ready with the first draft of a service for authorization or commendation, it will submit the draft to the House of Bishops. Formally, it is for the House of Bishops to order the introduction of liturgical business into the Synod. Experience over thirty years has shown that it is desirable that a draft service should be introduced into the Synod only if there is broad general support for the draft among members of the House. The custom now is that the draft is presented to the House by the Commission's chairman (if, as now, he is a member of it) or by a bishop who is a member. The bishops generally are then invited to submit comments, criticism and suggestions in writing to a committee of four or five of the House, appointed *ad hoc* but always including two bishops who are members of the Commission.

The Bishops' Committee meets to distil and evaluate their colleagues' comments; and in the light of their appraisal the Committee confers with members of the Liturgical Commission who have been particularly concerned with the draft. The aim is to secure, out of these consultations, a text which is acceptable equally to the Commission and to the bishops. Consultation will continue, if need be, as long as required to reach consensus.

Once the Bishops' approval is given the draft goes to the General Synod. If the draft is to be considered for (full) authorization by the Synod, the Synod's Appointments Sub-

Committee will designate two or three of the Commission members who have Synod seats, together with one or two Synod members *not* on the Commission, to form the Steering Committee of members in charge to pilot the draft through the Synod.

If the Synod carries the motion for general consideration the Measure is then usually referred to a Revision Committee. The chairman and members of the Steering Committee are members of the Revision Committee *ex officio*. A majority of the members of the Revision Committee (including its chairman) will be Synod members who belong neither to the Steering Committee nor to the Commission. They, like the Steering Committee members, will be appointed by the Appointments Sub-Committee. It is then open to Synod members and, if they wish, to others to send in suggestions for amendment of the text. Synod members who make proposals are entitled as of right to attend the Revision Committee to put their case for their amendment(s). Decisions are taken, after debate, by simple majority of the (full) Revision Committee. The amended draft is then returned to the Synod. At that stage members can only raise matters which have first been aired (and rejected) by the Revision Committee. In considering the draft at this stage the Synod will customarily have a report of the text showing clearly the amendments which have been made. It will also have a report, drafted and marshalled by the Committee's secretary, which will record all the amendments put to the Committee, with brief indications as to why particular proposals were rejected.

It is open to the full Synod to review 'on revision' any matter considered and decided by the Revision Committee. The final stage of authorization is for the Synod to give final approval to the draft and to determine the period for which it is to be authorized. Before the draft is considered for final approval, it is referred to the House of Bishops. Theoretically the House of Bishops at that stage can make any change it chooses in the text. In its origin, the purpose of the power was, and remains, to enable the bishops finally to satisfy themselves of the doctrinal soundness of the draft in the form which it has finally taken. But it also gives an opportunity for the refinement and 'polishing' of the rough edges which remain after the process of synodical amendments. It is for the Steering Committee and the Liturgical Commission to advise the House of Bishops on these points.

Are present procedures satisfactory?

Over the years since 1965, when the present phase of liturgical revision effectively began, voices have constantly been raised against a system which gives to a body of more than five hundred people the right to scrutinize and directly to alter and amend the texts of drafts if these are alternative to the services in the 1662 Book. What the Synod does, under the present system, is to treat liturgical texts very much as it treats draft legislation. Any Synod member, however liturgically uninformed, can suggest an amendment. The detailed process of revision goes to a revision committee, many of whose members (the critics say) may be singularly ill-informed. Surely, the argument runs, it is wrong to put carefully considered liturgical texts, prepared by experts, through so crude a process? Instances can be quoted where the synodical process has produced forms of words which are unsatisfactory both in the meaning which they convey and also in the actual speaking of them by priest and people. Others have pointed to the time consuming nature of the method: one thousand amendments were submitted at the revision stage of what is now Rite A. These arguments come together: would it not be better, and make for better liturgy, to place actual final decision-taking in expert hands, even if at stages comment is invited from the General Synod or more widely?

But the origin of the present arrangements lies in the

reluctance of Parliament — and of the synodical laity — to allow responsibility for liturgical matters to rest upon a small group of experts, or even upon the bishops, or the general body of bishops and clergy. When the work on *ASB 1980* was complete liturgists, longing for a simpler system and one more readily attuned to expert guidance, sat down with experts in the General Synod's Standing Orders to see if a better way could be found. It became clear, however, that the Synod was not prepared to see its powers cut down: all that emerged, in effect, were a few minor improvements designed to ease the process of tidying and polishing after the process of amendment and before final approval. Accordingly, the process, as it has operated since 1966, remains substantially in force so far as alternatives to the Book of Common Prayer are concerned. In developing the process of *commendation* — rather than authorization — forms of service which are *not* BCP alternatives, the House of Bishops has met, in relation to these forms of services, the criticisms of those who dislike the amendment of liturgical texts 'on the floor' of the Synod.

The *ASB 1980* is due for major revision in the period leading up to the year 2000. Is there any possibility that the House of Bishops — or the Synod itself — might go further and extend the procedures which govern the new-style process of 'commendation' to apply also to the authorization of alternatives to BCP and ASB? As matters stand in 1989, there seems no likelihood that the Synod will relax its direct involvement and control, even assuming that Parliament would allow it. There are many factors, some to do with politics and churchmanship, which militate against any such relaxation.

But is the process of involving the whole Synod as unfortunate as some critics suggest? Many people, looking back, feel that the original Series Three modern language Communion Service was a low point in the process of moving towards *ASB 1980*. The bishops, recognizing that it would have to be revised before going into *ASB 1980*, instructed the

Liturgical Commission to produce a revision of that service, in preparation for *ASB 1980*. Yet the Synod, with its one thousand amendments, were able to insist upon a major and more radical exercise. Ten years later, with the widespread acceptance of Rite A, this can be seen as a happy outcome. If it is, then can it not also be seen as a good and positive reason for keeping major liturgical matters in the Synod's hands? It is the old Church of England argument: the system is not perfect — but it works.

13

Postscript

DONALD GRAY

It is a fact that I am alone among the contributors to this book in being one of those who worked on many of the stages of the liturgical activity which preceded the publication in 1980 of The Alternative Service Book. The production of that book was, all but the more reactionary members of our Church must agree, a significant achievement for the work and mission of the Church of England. It was the result of many years of scholarship which was combined with an impressive accumulation of pastoral wisdom. Because of the latter it was, not surprisingly, much influenced by the changes that had taken place in the patterns of worship within the Church of England in the previous sixty years. If it seems as though a large proportion of the creative energy expended in the creation of the ASB was directed towards the revision of the eucharistic rite that is very understandable, because the single most obvious and urgent need of the Church for its week-by-week worship in the 1960s was such a revision of the Eucharist.

However, that is not to say that the revisers were not sensitive to the needs of the Church in its pastoral offices and for the daily Office; unfortunately the one and only item on the agenda at that time was 'Prayer Book Revision'. Such a priority does not necessarily produce the best forms for worship, devotion and pastoral ministrations that can be devised. It cannot be disputed that much devoted energy, together with years of accumulated academic expertise, were brought to bear on the resulting revision of the Prayer Book forms. Nevertheless, it must always be borne in mind when evaluating the ASB that there never was a wholesale deviation from that principle, which had been enshrined in the Liturgical Commission's *modus operandi* from its earliest days, in the work done up to the crucial date of 1980.

From the pages of this present work it can clearly be seen that there is a new wind blowing through the liturgical cloisters. It is generated not only by the recent quite considerable quickening of pace in liturgical scholarship and discovery and the sharing of that knowledge on a world-wide and ecumenical basis, but also by an evangelical zeal. *Faith in the City* and similar reports have made us uncomfortably aware that the forms and patterns which cradle-Anglicans have, perhaps too easily, accepted as the norm are exceedingly blunt instruments of evangelism when placed in the hands of those who have the task of proclaiming the gospel to an increasingly indifferent and sometimes even hostile world.

The worship of the Church and the performance of its pastoral ministrations are still the most visible points at which the Church reveals its public face. If this worship and these ceremonies are to speak convincingly of God's continuing love for individuals as well as his caring concern for the world of his creation, then they must be as accessible as it is humanly possible to devise, while still retaining echoes and nuances which evoke the infinite and eternal. To shackle the mission of the Church with forms which are inherited from merely one stage in the history of the pilgrimage of the Christian Church is just as surely to shackle the Spirit.

Any Prayer Book which is designed for the Year of Our Lord 2000 must of necessity be two-eyed. It must have one eye fixed on the splendours and the glories of the traditions of Christian liturgical worship and devotion all down the ages; while at the same time making absolutely sure that the other is resolutely focused on our God-given task of making the gospel both alive and available in his world of the present moment. We, the authors of this collection, invite you to join with us in beginning, even now, on a venture of exploration which is decisively aimed at that goal.